HISTORY DETECTIVES

Modern
Weapons

HIST⊙RY DETECTIVES

Modern
Weapons

Discover the technology of war from 1700 to the present day

Will Fowler

southwater

This edition is published by Southwater

© Anness Publishing Limited 2000, 2003

Southwater is an imprint of Anness Publishing Ltd
Hermes House, 88–89 Blackfriars Road, London SE1 8HA
tel. 020 7401 2077; fax 020 7633 9499
www.southwaterbooks.com; info@anness.com

This edition distributed in the UK by The Manning
Partnership Ltd, 6 The Old Dairy, Melcombe Road, Bath
BA2 3LR; tel. 01225 478 444; fax 01225 478 440;
sales@manning-partnership.co.uk

This edition distributed in the USA and Canada by National Book
Network, 4501 Forbes Boulevard, Suite 200, Lanham, MD 20706;
tel. 301 459 3366; fax 301 429 5746; www.nbnbooks.com

This edition distributed in Australia by Pan Macmillan Australia,
Level 18, St Martins Tower,
31 Market St, Sydney, NSW 2000;
tel. 1300 135 113; fax 1300 135 103;
customer.service@macmillan.com.au

This edition distributed in New Zealand by
The Five Mile Press (NZ) Ltd, PO Box 33–1071 Takapuna,
Unit 11/101–111 Diana Drive, Glenfield, Auckland 10;
tel. (09) 444 4144; fax (09) 444 4518; fivemilenz@xtra.co.nz

Publisher: Joanna Lorenz
Senior Editor: Lisa Miles
Art Director: Clare Sleven
Project Editors: Neil de Cort and Cindy Leaney
Assistant Editors: Simon Nevill and Helen Parker
Design: Casebourne Rose Design Associates
Production Controller: Rachel Jones
Art Commissioning: Susanne Bull, Lynne French
Picture Research: Lesley Cartlidge; Libbe Mella
Kate Miles; Janice Bracken

Previously published as *Exploring History: Modern Weapons and Warfare*

Picture Credits
The publishers would like to thank the following
artists who have contributed to this book:
Mike White (Temple Rogers); Richard Hook (Linden Artists);
Rob Sheffield; John Woodcock; Wayne Ford; Andrew Robinson;
Martin Sanders; Mike Taylor.
Maps: Roger Stewart.
Special thanks to Peter Sarson.

The publishers wish to thank the following
for supplying photographs for this book:
Page 14 (BL) Solo Syndication Ltd.; 17 (BC) Popper-Handke Collection;
20 (BR) Science Photo Library; 31 (BC) Imperial War Museum; 46 (CR)
Popperfoto; 53 (BC) Popperfoto.

Special thanks to Will Fowler for supplying the following images:
Page 7 (CL); 9 (TR, C); 10 (BR); 12 (BC, BR); 13 (TL); 14 (BR); 15 (CR); 16
(C); 17 (TL, CR, BL); 18 (TL, BR); 20 (C); 21 (CR); 22 (CR); 24 (TL, CR,
BL, BR); 25 (CL, BL, BC); 26 (C); 27 (TL, BL); 28 (CL, BL, BR); 29 (CR,
BL); 30 (TR); 31 (TL, TR, BL); 32 (CR); 33 (BL); 34 (BL, BR); 35 (BL); 36
(TL); 37 (TL); 43 (BL); 46 (CR, BC, TL, BR); 50 (BR); 51 (CL, BL); 54
(C, BR, BL); 56 (BR); 58 (BR); 61 (TL, BC).
All other pictures from Dover Publications and Miles Kelly archives.

1 3 5 7 9 10 8 6 4 2

The measurements for weapons and ammunition used throughout
this book vary between imperial and metric according
to the manufacturers' specifications.

CONTENTS

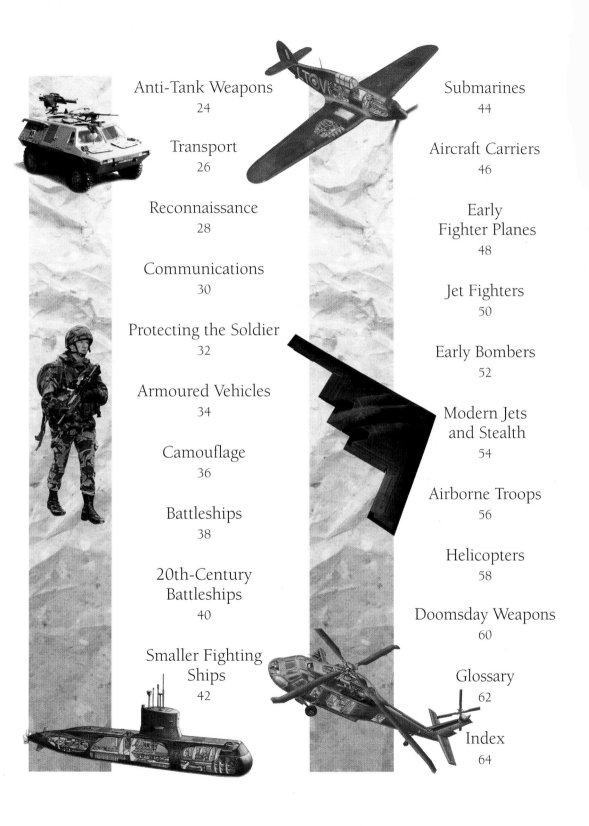

ntroduction

BETWEEN THE YEAR 1700 AND THE PRESENT DAY, the ways that wars are conducted has changed beyond all recognition. Flintlock muskets have been replaced by automatic machine guns, and horses have been replaced by armoured tanks and assault helicopters. Change has been most rapid in the last hundred years. World War I was fought mostly hand-to-hand, but the main battles of the Gulf War were fought by missiles and planes.

The introduction of steam power and petrol engines meant that soldiers did not have to rely on animals for transport, which could get tired or injured. The ships which relied on the wind for power, were replaced by vessels that moved at greater speeds against winds and currents when powered by steam.

Armor plating which protected knights in the Middle Ages, found new uses protecting ships, land vehicles, and even aircraft. New lighter, stronger, and even fire-resistant materials were developed. These new materials were initially used to provide clothing to protect crews, but were later also used for fire fighters and the emergency services.

Before the World War I people were optimistic about science. They believed that technological advances would make life safer, healthier, and easier. In part this has been true, but science has also been used for war. Destruction on a huge scale has now become a reality. But though the two world wars led to the development of weapons of mass destruction (nuclear, chemical, and biological weapons), they were also the spur for life-saving medical techniques.

▲ RIFLES
Ever since they were invented in the 19th century, rifles have played a critical role in warfare.

▼ KEY DATES
The panel charts the development of modern weapons, from Leonardo da Vinci's sketches of a helicopter, to the introduction of stealth technology in modern aircraft.

▼ FORTIFICATIONS
As the technology of warfare has developed, the means of defending against ever-changing weaponry have altered dramatically.

PISTOLS AND ARTILLERY

The Gatling gun

- **1784** Invention of the shrapnel shell
- **1807** Forsyth patents the percussion ignition.
- **1835** Lefaucheux patents the pin-fire cartridge.
- **1835** Colt patents his revolver design.
- **1883** Maxim patents fully automatic machine gun.

- **1901** British 10-pounder cannon introduced.
- **1914–1918** World War I: long-range artillery in use
- **1934** First general-purpose machine gun introduced
- **1939–1945** World War II: self-loading rifle developed. Recoilless guns, rocker artillery, and anti-tank guns in use
- **1947** Kalashnikov designs the AK47 assault rifle.
- **1957** Italian 105mm Model 56 pack howitzer appears.

Colt automatic pistol

FIGHTING ON THE LAND

- **1850** Morse Code invented
- **1858** First aerial photography
- **1865** First antiseptics used
- **1882** Armored steel developed
- **1914–1918** World War I: land and sea camouflage developed
- **1916** September: first tanks used in World War I
- **1925** French demonstrate the half-track vehicle
- **1939–1945** World War II: aerial photography and infrared technology developed
- **1943** Infrared night-vision viewer used

- **1944–1945** German missiles launched against Britain
- **1944** June 6: D-Day, the largest amphibious operation in history, takes place
- **1957** First space satellite launched
- **1991** Iraqi SCUD surface-to-surface missiles launched in the Gulf War

World War II Sherman tank

▼ AVIATION
The development of military air power has been one of the most important changes to modern warfare. Controlling the skies above any battlefield has become critical to modern tactics and critical to military success. Aircraft are now more deadly than ever. They can fly faster and for longer, and over greater distances, carrying more weaponry than ever before.

From the 1940s saw the rapid development of the airplane as the jet turbine replaced the piston engine. New planes could fly further and with more weapons than ever before.

Radio communications began at the end of the 1800s as a laboratory experiment. One hundred years later it had become an essential part of the equipment of war. The world wars showed how important communication was, and scientists developed the technology to meet the demands of soldiers.

Helicopters had existed in a basic form before World War II, but by 1945, engineers in the United States and Britain were designing new, more powerful versions of these rotary wing craft. By the end of the 1900s the helicopter had become a life saver, lifting sailors from the sea or survivors from burning buildings.

The soldiers of the developed world are no longer troops sent to fight. They have become peacekeepers, attempting to prevent brutal wars. Fast communications allow them to keep their national leaders informed about developments on the ground on an hour-by-hour basis.

▲ MOBILITY
The ability to move large numbers of troops and equipment quickly and easily is an essential p(of any successful campaign.

▼ TECHNOLOGY
Warfare has always pushed back technologic(boundaries, from the first tanks to stealth bombers like this B2 bomber.

FIGHTING ON THE SEAS

- **1805** Battle of Trafalgar
- **1863** The steam-driven submersible *David* attacks Federal ironclad ship
- **1904** *Aigret*, first diesel-powered boat
- **1906** Launch of H.M.S. *Dreadnought*
- **1914–1918** World War I
- **1916** May 31: Battle of Jutland
- **1939–1945** German U-boats use "wolf pack" tactics against Allied shipping
- **1941** May 27: sinking of the *Bismarck*
- **1942** June 4–7: Battle of Midway

- **1944** June 6: D-Day
- **1954** *U.S.S. Nautilus*, the first nuclear-powered submarine, is commissioned
- **1961** *U.S.S. Enterprise* is first nuclear-powered carrier
- **1966** Soviet Osa-class missile-armed craft enter service
- **1990-1991** Osa-class craft see action in the Gulf War

U.S. Knox-class frigate

REACHING FOR THE SKIES

F86 Sabre

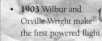

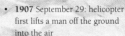

- **1903** Wilbur and Orville Wright make the first powered flight
- **1907** September 29: helicopter first lifts a man off the ground into the air
- **1912** Machine gun fired from aircraft for first time
- **1914–1918** World War I
- **1914** October 5: first aircraft to be shot down
- **1939–1945** World War II: first strategic bombing
- **1945** August 6 and 9: atomic bombs dropped on Japan
- **1945** December 3: the first jet landing and takeoff from an aircraft carrier

- **1950** First jet-versus-jet victory in the Korean War
- **1951** Canberra bomber is the first jet to fly across the North Atlantic nonstop
- **1955** B-52 enters service with the United States Air Force
- **1977** December: first flight of Lockheed Martin F-117
- **1989** July 17: first flight of Northrop Grumman B-2A Spirit stealth aircraft
- **1991** February 24: 300 helicopters used in Gulf War in the largest aerial assault in the history of aviation

Pistols and Rifles

▲ RIFLEMAN
A 19th-century French soldier carries a bolt-action rifle.

Y OU CAN SEE PISTOLS every day in most countries because police officers carry them. In thrillers and westerns, the heroes and villains are usually armed with pistols. You have probably seen lots of pistols, but do you know how they work?

There are two sorts of pistols. A revolver has a cylindrical magazine with six rounds of bullets. Newer pistols are self-loading, with a detachable box magazine that fits into the handle and can hold up to 14 rounds of ammunition. Rifles are bolt-action, semi-automatic, or automatic weapons, and have a magazine that holds between 5 and 30 rounds. An automatic weapon automatically places the next round in the chamber for firing, so fires repeatedly when the trigger is pulled.

▶ RIFLES
British soldiers of the late 19th century use their massed firepower to compensate for the short range and inaccuracy of their flintlock muskets.

The most famous revolvers are the "Six Guns" used in the 1800s in the United States. These were famous as they enabled the user to fire six shots in quick succession. In World War I (1914–1918) and World War II (1939–1945), British troops used the .455inch Webley MarkVI revolver or the .38inch Enfield Number 2 Mark1.

The Germans used the Luger pistol as it was easy to reload. It was named after Georg Luger, a designer at the Ludwig Löwe arms factory in Berlin. It weighed 2lbs, had an eight-shot magazine and fired a .36inch round.

The U.S. Army carried the .45inch Colt 1911 self-loading pistol throughout both world wars, the Korean War, and the Vietnam War. It weighs 2¾ lbs. and has a seven-round magazine. The Belgian 9mm Browning High Power was first manufactured in 1935. It weighs 2½ lbs. when loaded and has an effective range of 55–80 yards. Its magazine holds 13 rounds in two staggered rows—a feature copied in later designs.

The British used the bolt-action .303inch Short Magazine Lee Enfield (SMLE) rifle during World War I

A SOLDIER'S TOOLS

The rifle and pistol have always been the tools of the infantryman. They are light and portable, and have become more accurate and faster firing. Cavalry, artillery, and support troops such as engineers also carry these weapons, primarily for self-protection rather than attack. The rifle and pistol cartridge have also allowed the weapons' mechanical feed to be improved.

▲ THE U.S. ARMY RIFLE
In the years before the Civil War, the U.S. Army used a .58inch rifle. Rifling made the bullet more accurate by spinning it, causing the bullet to fly straighter. The bayonet was used in close-quarter fighting.

▲ SHORT MAGAZINE LEE ENFIELD (SMLE) BOLT-ACTION RIFLE
The compact bolt-action rifle was 45¼ inches long, weighed 10lbs. and had a ten-round magazine. It was used by the British Army from 1907 to 1943. More than three million were made in Britain, India, and Australia.

▲ BOLT ACTION
The Mauser action had five rounds. They could be loaded into the breech, the back part, by moving the bolt.

▲ THE AUTOMATIC
The U.S. Colt 1911A1 (right) and Browning 1903 are two classic self-loading pistols. Their ammunition is in a magazine in the pistol grip.

▲ THE M16
The M16 is now widely used throughout the world. It was first used by the US Army in Vietnam. At that time the M16 was revolutionary because it fired a .22inch round, was made from plastics and alloys and weighed only 8lbs.

and for much of World War II. The German .31inch Karabiner 98K was a very accurate weapon but only had only a five-round magazine. The U.S. Garand M1 rifle and M1 carbine were popular self-loading rifles during World War II as they were tough and reliable.

Two weapons have dominated armed conflicts since 1945; the U.S. .22 inch M16 Armalite rifle weighing 9lbs., and the Soviet-designed .3inch AK47 weighing 10¾ lbs. Both can fire on full automatic at 700 (M16) and 600 (AK47) rounds per minute (rpm).

▲ THE ENFIELD L85A1 RIFLE
This is the current rifle issued to British troops. It weighs 8¾lbs. and is 31½ inches long. On automatic it fires .22inch rounds at 700 rounds per minute (rpm). The Enfield L85A1 has been used in action in the Persian Gulf, in Kosovo, and in Northern Ireland.

▼ THE SNIPER'S HIDE
In World War II, snipers built camouflaged positions called hides in which they could observe and shoot at the enemy. They were often concealed for long periods in the hides, which needed to be well built and weatherproof. This hide has is covered in turf.

A turf roof conceals the hide.

The hide is deep enough to allow the sniper to stand.

▲ THE SNIPER
A soldier is camouflaged to blend into the woodland. He aims his Accuracy International L96A1 .30inch sniper's rifle. It is fitted with an optical sight.

Key Dates

- 1807 Dr. Forsyth patents the percussion ignition.
- 1812 Pauly patents the first cartridge breech-loader.
- 1835 Lefaucheux patents the pin-fire cartridge.
- 1835 Colt patents his revolver design.
- 1849 The Minié rifle replaces smooth-bore rifles.
- 1886 French adopt the first small-bore smokeless-powder cartridge.
- 1888 Britain adopts Lee–Metford bolt-action repeater.
- 1939–1945 Self-loading rifle developed.

Automatic Weapons

▲ THE GARDNER
This early water-cooled, hand-cranked machine gun is mounted on an adjustable tripod. Its ammunition is fed into the chamber from the top.

THE FIRST MACHINE GUN dates back to 1718, when Puckle's gun was developed in Britain. It was a large hand-cranked revolver on a stand that fired seven rounds per minute (rpm). The Gatling gun was also hand-cranked. It fired at a rate of 100–200rpm. It was developed in the United States in 1862 and used in the Civil War.

The first successful automatic machine gun was the .32inch Maxim gun designed by the American Hiram Maxim. It used the energy of the exploding cartridges to operate the mechanism and fired at 500rpm. This rapid firing rate heated up the barrel, so it was cooled by a water-filled jacket. The British used the Maxim gun in action in 1895.

The French Hotchkiss machine gun used the gases of the exploding cartridges to operate its mechanism. It had a heavier barrel designed not to need a water jacket, but which

cooled in the air. Ammunition was fed in on a cloth belt, where other similar weapons used metal belts.

The belt-fed British Vickers .303inch machine gun was designed in 1891 and was not withdrawn from service with the British Army until 1963. The World War II German MG42 was a .32inch general-purpose machine gun (GPMG). Stamping and spot welding speeded its manufacturing process. It had a top range of 6,560 feet and fired 1,550rpm. Features of its design were copied in the postwar Belgian FN MAG and in the U.S. M60 machine guns.

The first submachine guns (SMGs) fired

◄ THE GATLING GUN
The hand-cranked Gatling gun, used here by British soldiers, was introduced in 1862. Designed by Dr. Richard Gatling, it had between six and ten barrels. It saw action in the Civil War and was later adopted by the U.S. Army during the Spanish-American War. Later models were mounted on a light artillery carriage.

SUBMACHINE GUNS (SMGS)
The first submachine gun to go into service was the Italian Villar Perosa, which was used in World War I. SMGs fire pistol-caliber ammunition such as .45inch at the same rate as a conventional machine gun. They are not accurate over long ranges but are ideal in situations where intense close-range firepower is required.

► THE STEN MK II SMG
This .36in SMG weighs 7½lbs empty and fires at 550rpm. More than two million were made in World War II.

◄ THE AK47
The AK47 assault rifle fires a .30inch round, which is halfway between a rifle round and a pistol round.

◄ THE TOMMY GUN
The Thompson M1 was the simplified World War II version of this SMG. It had a 30-round box magazine and weighed 12lbs. empty.

► THE UZI SMG
The Uzi is a .36inch SMG developed in Israel. It weighs 8¾lbs. empty and fires at a rate of 600r.p.m.

pistol-sized ammunition and could be carried by one person. They were developed at the end of World War I. The .45inch Thompson (Tommy) gun, designed in the 1920s in the United States, became notorious in the gang wars of the 1920s. It was widely used by British and American troops in World War II.

The World War II German MP38/40 was the first submachine gun to have a folding metal butt. This feature reduced its size from 33 inches down to $25\frac{1}{4}$ inches. It fired at 500rpm. and had a thirty-round magazine.

Modern SMGs are compact and lightweight weapons. They are a common weapon for bodyguards as they can be carried inside jackets or briefcases.

▲ HELICOPTERMOUNTED
Machine guns were first fitted to helicopters by the French in the 1960s. They are now used by helicopters to protect the aircraft when flying into "hot" landing zones or to attack enemy infantry.

▲ VEHICLE MOUNTED
A Belgian .30inch MAG machine gun is mounted on a vehicle in the desert. The MAG is in service in many countries and can be mounted on a tripod for long-range fire, or on a built-in bipod for shorter ranges.

▶ THE M60
The poor reliability of the U.S. .30inch M60 general-purpose machine gun in Vietnam earned it the nickname "the Pig." It has since been modified and improved and is widely used around the world.

▼ BEATEN ZONE
A machine gun fires long bursts over long ranges, spreading its bullets into a cone-shaped area called a "beaten zone." It is fatal or very risky for soldiers to enter this bullet-swept zone.

Machine guns are very effective defense weapons when used in pairs. Two machine guns can be positioned so that they fire from the side across the path of an aproaching enemy. This arrangement makes their fire overlap, creating two overlapping "beaten zones." This combined fire power creates a doubly dangerous area for the enemy.

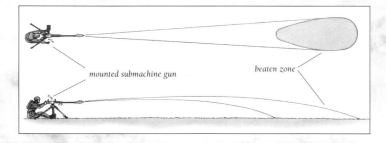

mounted submachine gun

beaten zone

Key Dates

- 1883 Maxim patents fully automatic machine gun.

- 1896 United States orders Browning-Colt gas-operated gun.

- 1926 Czech ZB/vz26 light machine gun designed.

- 1934 MG34 introduced, the first general-purpose machine gun .

- 1942 MG42 creates the basis for many postwar designs.

- 1947 Kalashnikov designs the AK47 assault rifle.

- 1961 U.S. Army evaluates Armalite rifle.

Artillery—Cannons and Mortars

ATTLES IN EUROPE and North America between the 1500s and 1800s were thundering smoke-filled affairs, as artillery soldiers manned their cannons and each side bombarded the other.

Cannons were loaded from the muzzle (front end) and fired round shot or cannonballs. The major development in artillery weapons came with the introduction of rifled barrels in 1858. A rifled barrel makes a shell spin in flight, and so it is more accurate. Breech loading—loading the gun from the back—was introduced in around 1870. Recoil mechanisms to absorb the "kick" of the firing followed in 1888.

▼ RAPID-FIRE CANNON

These cannons were mounted on warships or used for close-range coastal defense. They entered service in the late 19th century. Improved recoil mechanisms permitted the gun to remain stable while firing. The crew were protected by an armored shield, but in later years they would be enclosed in a turret.

▼ DESERT FIREPOWER

A howitzer is an artillery piece designed to fire at a steep angle, usually over fortifications. This is a U.S. M198 155mm howitzer in action during the Gulf War of 1990–1991. It entered service with the U.S. Army and U.S. Marine Corps in 1979. The howitzer weighs 7,163kg and has a crew of 11. It has a maximum range of 59,530feet with standard ammunition, but this increases to 98,400m with a rocket-assisted projectile (RAP).

BIG BOYS

Before aircraft that could drop large bomb loads had been developed, artillery was used to bombard fortifications or defend important locations such as ports and capital cities. The bigger the caliber (diameter of the barrel), the bigger the shell and so the greater the volume of explosives that could be enclosed in the gun. Big shells were therefore more destructive.

▶ U.S. ARMY BREECH-LOADING HOWITZER
This siege howitzer is mounted on a turntable and has a hoist for loading.

▲ RAILGUNS
Railroads have been used to carry heavy guns and mortars since the Civil War. The world's biggest guns were the German guns that were used in World War II.

▼ MODERN MORTAR
A soldier loads a British 3¼ inch mortar with a high-explosive (HE) bomb. On the left a second soldier kneels ready with another bomb to ensure a rapid rate of fire.

▲ SELF-PROPELLED GUNS
*The U.S. 6¹/2 inch M109 SP gun (above) and the
U.S. 8 inch M110A SP howitzer (right: side and
top-down views). The tracked chassis gives
them greater mobility on the battlefield.*

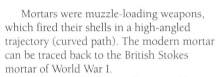

Mortars were muzzle-loading weapons,
which fired their shells in a high-angled
trajectory (curved path). The modern mortar
can be traced back to the British Stokes
mortar of World War I.

Modern artillery ranges from World War II
weapons, such as the huge German railway siege
guns—the 32inch K(E) Gustav bombarded Sevastopol
and Leningrad—to the tiny Japanese 2³/4 inch battalion
gun Type 92. The K(E) Gustav fired a 12,000lb. shell to
29 miles. It had a crew of 1,500 men. The Japanese
gun, with a crew of five, fired a 9¹/4lb. shell to 4,500feet.

World War II mortars included the massive German
24 inch Karl, which was also used to bombard
Sevastopol, as well as Warsaw. It fired a 3940lb. shell to

a maximum range of 7,300 feet. It was mounted on a
tracked chassis, but this gave it very limited mobility
and it crawled along at only 6mph. Karl mortars had a
crew of 18. There was also the little British 2inch
mortar. It weighed 10¹/4lb., fired a 2¹/2lb. bomb to a
maximum range of 1,496 feet and had crew of two.

Future artillery designs may include a 6¹/4inch
howitzer built with new materials that is as light as a
4¹/4inch weapon. Shells will soon be guided and
capable of changing their path during flight.

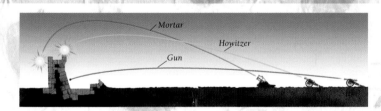

▲ TRAJECTORIES
Mortars and howitzers have a
high-angled trajectory and can
lob shells over obstacles. Field
artillery has a flatter trajectory.

▶ INDIRECT FIRE
An artillery battery may not see
its target when it fires. It can be
instructed to adjust its fire by
an observer who watches where
the shells fall.

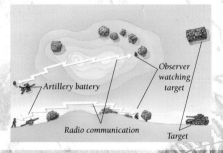

Key Dates

- 1784 Invention of the Shrapnel shell.
- 1858 French adopt rifled artillery.
- 1870 Breech loading widely used.
- 1884 French develop smokeless gunpowder.
- 1888 Konrad Hausser develops long-recoil cylinder.
- 1899 Maxim "Pom Pom" automatic cannon in use.
- 1914–1918 World War I: long-range artillery developed.
- 1939–1945 World War II: recoilless guns, rocker artillery, and anti-tank guns.

Artillery—Pack Guns

In July 1999 the last Royal Tournament was held in London. It marked the end of the annual British Royal Navy field gun race between crews from Portsmouth and Plymouth. The crews dismantled a Victorian 10-pounder mountain gun and raced across a series of obstacles then re-assembled it and fired a blank shell. It was an exciting test of strength and coordination. Pack howitzers like the 10-pounder were designed to be dismantled and carried by men or five mules across mountainous or rough terrain. If the pack artillery could then be assembled on a mountain ridge, their fire could dominate the roads through the valleys below.

The 10-pounder was used in India on the Northwest Frontier between 1901 and 1915.

▲ FIELD PIECE
Horse-drawn artillery consisted of the gun, the limber that contained the ammunition and charges, and the team of horses.

▶ ITALIAN PACK GUNS
Alpine mountain troops move their guns to new positions in World War I. Pack guns could be broken down into about four sections for ease of transportation.

It fired a 11¼lb. shell out to 18,000 feet. The gun became famous as the "screw gun" because its barrel broke down into two sections that were screwed together when it was assembled for firing.

The 10-pounder was replaced by the 3.7inch pack howitzer which soldiered on during both world wars. The howitzer's maximum weight was 5,500lbs., and it fired a 22¾lb. shell out to 18,000 feet.

MOVING AROUND
Pack howitzers, or mountain artillery, and light anti-aircraft guns were designed to be dismantled so that they could be carried by troops or mules to remote mountaintop positions. Today's light guns can be carried by helicopter, which is faster and more reliable.

◀ MUSCLE POWER
Royal Navy sailors at the Royal Tournament in London, demonstrating how the British 10-pounder mountain gun can be dismantled and reassembled.

▲ ANTIAIRCRAFT GUN
A Soviet-made, Iraqi ZPU-4 1 inch antiaircraft gun in a coastal position. It was captured in 1991 in Kuwait at the end of the Gulf War.

good that it has been effectively copied in India with a 3 inch pack gun howitzer. The Model 56 can be broken down into 11 parts which can be transported by mules or even carried on soldiers' backs for short distances. It weighs 3225lbs. and can fire a 47½lb. high-explosive shell out to 34,770 feet.

The use of helicopters and the widespread need for air mobility make the requirement for light guns and pack howitzers almost universal. They can be transported slung beneath helicopters and brought into action very quickly.

The guns of the future will be constructed from new materials, many of which are currently used in modern aircraft design. These materials are strong but much lighter than steel and alloys.

▲ CIVIL WAR CANNON
The breech-loading cannon used in the 1860s in the United States were very similar to those used during the Napoleonic Wars.

During World War II, the U.S. 75mm M1A1 pack howitzer proved a very effective weapon for airborne forces. It was originally designed for carriage by six mules. The M1A1 fired a 6.24kg high-explosive shell out to 29,290 feet and weighed 588.3kg. The 105mm M3 howitzer was a bigger version of the M1A1 and weighed 1132.7kg. It could fire a 14.98kg shell out to 21,760 feet.

Postwar mountain artillery has been dominated by the Italian OTO Melara 105/14 Model 56 4.2inch howitzer. It was introduced in 1957, and since then more than 2,500 have been built. The Model 56 has been used by more than 17 countries. Its design is so

▲ PACK HOWITZER
The Italian 4¹/₅inch Model 56 pack howitzer in action. The shield can be removed to save weight. The howitzer's hinged trail legs can be folded, which makes the gun easier to transport.

▼ ANTIAIRCRAFT FIRE
Antiaircraft gun crews developed the skill of aiming just in front of a moving aircraft. This meant that the shell, with its time fuse, exploded as the plane flew into the blast and fragments. Radar now makes the job faster and easier.

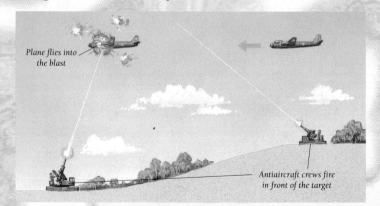

Plane flies into the blast

Antiaircraft crews fire in front of the target

Key Dates

- 1901 British 10-pounder introduced.

- 1901–1915 The 10-pounder used on Indian Northwest Frontier.

- 1914–1918 World War I: antiaircraft guns used.

- 1932 Swedish 1½ inch Bofors antiaircraft gun appears.

- 1936 German 3½ inch Flak 36 anti-aircraft gun developed.

- 1939–1945 World War II: U.S. 75mm M1A1 pack howitzer used.

- 1957 Italian 4½ inch Model 56 pack howitzer appears.

Bombs, Rockets, and Torpedoes

ROCKETS PROPELLED by gunpowder are a common sight in the United States on the Fourth of July and in Britain on November 5 (Guy Fawkes' Night). People watch as the rockets streak into the sky and burst into a shower of colored stars. Rockets were originally used by the ancient Chinese as a weapon. They called them "fire arrows."

▲ TRENCH WARS
British troops on the Western Front in World War I, with a stock of mortars.

Later, in the 1800s, the British employed rockets against the French during the Napoleonic Wars. They were used in 1815 by a Royal Artillery troop at the Battle of Waterloo. American and European armies experimented with them throughout the 1800s.

▶ STINGER SAM
The U.S. low-altitude surface-to-air missile (SAM) has a maximum range of about 13,120 feet and a maximum speed of Mach 2.2. It has a $6\frac{1}{2}$lb. high-explosive warhead.

The self-propelled, or "fish," torpedo, developed in the late 1800s, revolutionized naval warfare. In World War I rockets were fitted to British fighter planes to attack German Zeppelin airships.

The first aerial bombs were used in World War I when pilots threw hand grenades at enemy troops. By the end of the war British bombers, such as the Handley Page 0/400, were carrying 1500lb. bombs to attack targets in Germany.

From World War II to the present day, bombs have been either high-explosive (HE) or incendiary devices. HE bombs are designed to explode on the surface or to penetrate reinforced concrete. Incendiary bombs burn at great heat and include napalm, a jellied fuel that splashes over a wide area. Cluster bombs are small HE bombs that are scattered from a larger container over a much wider area.

World War II rockets included the huge liquid-fuel German V-2, which was designed by Werner von Braun.

FLYING BOMBS

Aircraft and artillery use rockets and bombs to deliver high-explosive or incendiary payloads to target areas. Torpedoes launched from ships and submarines or dropped from the air proved very effective against ships of all sizes in World War II. Rockets have become a more effective weapon and are now launched from helicopters as well as from ships.

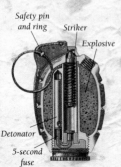

◀ HAND GRENADE
The British 36 grenade was introduced in 1915. It uses a mechanism with two safety features; a pin and also a handle.

Safety pin and ring   *Striker*
Explosive
Detonator
5-second fuse

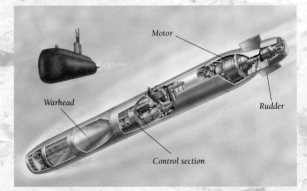

Motor
Warhead
Rudder
Control section

▲ TORPEDO
A torpedo consists of a warhead, fuel supply, motor, and rudder. Modern weapons also have wire guidance systems and warheads like those of an anti-tank weapon. When the warhead explodes it can penetrate deep into a ship's hull.

◀ MULTIPLE ROCKET LAUNCHER
The U.S. Multiple Rocket Launcher System (MRLS) was used in action during the Gulf War of 1990–1991. Its tracked chassis allows it to move rapidly around the battlefield, and it can reload in a few minutes.

Warhead

Computer *Fuse*

▲ SMART BOMB
The U.S. Paveway laser-guided bomb follows the reflected laser energy bounced back from its target. Laser- guided bombs were first used in the Vietnam War.

It weighed 13.3 tons and had a range of more than 185 miles. Another World War II rocket was the crude but effective solid-fuel 8inch rocket projectile (RP) fired from Allied aircraft.

Postwar rockets include intercontinental guided missiles with nuclear warheads, air-to-air missiles for combat aircraft, and anti-tank missiles with ranges of between 9,840 and 16,400 feet.

Robert Whitehead and Giovanni Lupis developed the first torpedo in 1866. It took its name from a Caribbean electric-ray fish. Torpedo boats were designed to carry the new weapon, and ships designed to destroy torpedoes, known as "destroyers," were in turn developed. The torpedo

made battleships vulnerable to attack by smaller vessels and submarines. In World War II torpedoes were also launched from airplanes. Modern torpedoes, with sophisticated guidance systems and warheads, are still carried by submarines. Torpedoes are also designed to seek and destroy submarines.

▶ ANTIAIRCRAFT MISSILE
The British Rapier surface-to-air missile was first used during the Falklands War in 1982. It has a maximum speed of 2,132 feet per second and a range of 22,960 feet.

▶ ALFRED NOBEL
Swedish scientist Alfred Nobel (1833–1896) developed a range of high explosives. These included dynamite (1863) and nitrocellulose (1888), from which smokeless propellant was developed. Nobel's explosives changed warfare in the 20th century.

▲ CLUSTER BOMB
The cluster bomb unit (CBU) dropped from aircraft contains smaller bombs, or submunitions, which are ejected to scatter across the ground. The CBU is used against soldiers in open or unarmored vehicles.

Key Dates

- 1860–1880 Hale rockets in use in the United States and Britain.

- 1890 Whitehead develops torpedo.

- 1903 Russian rocket engineer Konstantin Tsiolkovsky develops liquid-fuel rockets.

- 1944–1945 German V-1 and V-2 cruise missiles and ballistic missiles launched against Britain.

- 1981–1986 Air-launched cruise missiles enter service with U.S. Air Force.

- 1991 Iraqi SCUD surface-to-surface missiles launched in the Gulf War.

Mines and Fortifications

▲ ANTI-TANK MINE
An Italian plastic-bodied anti-tank mine which could destroy a truck and cripple a tank or armored vehicle.

SINCE THE US CIVIL WAR mines have been used as part of defensive fortifications to create obstacles and defend positions. But they are a major problem in the developing world today as they have been laid by warring parties in civil wars, causing injury to innocent civilians

The first mines were used as long ago as the Civil War (1861–1865), but these were crude devices. In the same war trenches were employed in field fortifications for the first time.

The design of forts had changed with the development of gunpowder. They were now no longer built upward but outward, with bombardment- proof barracks and gun batteries. From the late 17th century the French military engineer Sébastien Vauban was a major influence. He designed

huge star-shaped fortresses which allowed artillery to be used effectively. He also developed siege techniques for attacking fortresses.

Concrete was developed in the 20th century and was quickly adopted for fortifications. Barbed wire was first used extensively in the Boer War (1899–1902). In World War I the trenches of the Western Front were made of concrete, barbed wire, and corrugated iron. They stretched from Switzerland to the English Channel. At the end of the war the Germans produced

▶ WORLD WAR I TRENCHES
Trenches were dug deep enough so that men could walk along them below ground level. When the soldiers needed to shoot, they climbed up onto the firing step. To prevent the trenches from collapsing they were reinforced with material called a revetment.

PROTECTION
Trenches and bunkers were first dug in the Civil War, although earthworks had been built in the Napoleonic Wars. In Britain the Victorians built coastal forts to protect key harbors.

By World War I, improved artillery and the introduction of large numbers of machine guns forced the infantry underground. Materials such as steel girders and concrete make modern defenses very strong.

▶ ANTI-TANK OBSTACLES
American soldiers stand among concrete anti-tank obstacles called "dragon's teeth." They were built by the Germans in World War II to protect the western borders of the Third Reich.

▼ TUNNELS
In the Vietnam War the Vietcong (North Vietnamese) used tunnels like this one for concealment and as protection from bombs and shellfire.

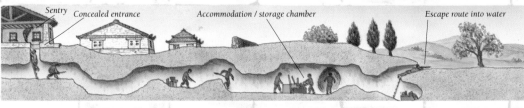

◀ PORTABLE DEFENSES
British soldiers deploy barbed wire in the desert in the Gulf War of 1990–1991. Barbed wire was first made in 1874. It is a portable, economical, and rapid form of perimeter defense used by armies around the world.

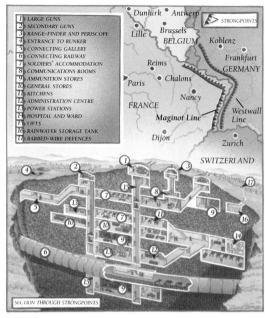

1. LARGE GUNS
2. SECONDARY GUNS
3. RANGE-FINDER AND PERISCOPE
4. ENTRANCE TO BUNKER
5. CONNECTING GALLERY
6. CONNECTING RAILWAY
7. SOLDIERS' ACCOMMODATION
8. COMMUNICATIONS ROOMS
9. AMMUNITION STORES
10. GENERAL STORES
11. KITCHENS
12. ADMINISTRATION CENTRE
13. POWER STATIONS
14. HOSPITAL AND WARD
15. LIFTS
16. RAINWATER STORAGE TANK
17. BARBED-WIRE DEFENCES

SECTION THROUGH STRONGPOINTS

▲ MAGINOT LINE
Built by the French before World War II, the Maginot Line was a series of fortifications 200 miles long, built to defend France's border with Germany. It took more than ten years to construct. It has been described as "a concrete battleship on land." Strongpoints in the Line had extra guns and equipment. They had underground tunnels and storage rooms, and air-conditioned barracks which protected against gas attacks. The fortifications included long-range artillery, mortars, and machine guns. When the Germans attacked, they outflanked the Maginot Line through neutral Belgium and Luxembourg.

the first anti-tank mines. They rigged standard artillery shells to explode when run over by a tank.

The two types of mine—anti-tank (AT) and anti-personnel (AP)—were developed in World War II. AT mines are designed to destroy trucks or to stop tanks by damaging their tracks or wheels. The German Teller AT mine contained 15lbs. of high explosive and has been the model for Russian and Israeli AT mines since 1945. AP mines kill or injure soldiers and civilians. Modern mines are made from plastic, which makes them almost impossible to detect. Techniques have been developed for detecting and clearing mines. Alternatively engineers may simply blast a path through a minefield.

In World War II lines of concrete fortifications were constructed, such as the coastal Atlantic Wall, built by the Germans, and the 200-mile-long Maginot Line, built by the French. However, the use of tanks and aircraft had made this kind of static defense outdated.

▲ ATLANTIC WALL
This German 6inch naval gun was part of a coastal defense battery at Longues-sur-Mer in Normandy, France. The slots on each side of the opening give the gun a wider range of movement.

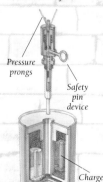

▼ AP MINE
The U.S. M16 jumping anti-personnel mine scatters metal pieces across 10–16 feet.

Pressure prongs

Safety pin device

Charge

Key Dates

- 1659 Vauban (1633–1707) devises new fortification systems to defeat artillery.
- 1861–1865 Civil War trench warfare near Richmond, Virginia.
- 1874 Barbed wire produced.
- 1899–1902 Boer War: first extensive use of barbed wire.
- 1904–1905 Russo-Japanese War.
- 1914–1918 World War I: fight for forts at Verdun.
- 1930s Construction of the Maginot Line and Westwall Line.
- 1942–1944 Construction of Atlantic Wall in World War II.

Guerrilla Warfare and Terrorism

▲ CHE GUEVARA
The Argentinian-born Cuban guerrilla leader was executed in Bolivia in 1967. Guevara was an icon for the young revolutionary movement during the 1960s.

EVEN DURING PEACETIME, terrorism is a threat on the streets of many cities and towns. Political groups and campaigners who have decided to break the law to further their aims use terrorism. They hope to frighten governments and the public into accepting their views. Together with revolutionary and guerrilla warfare, terrorism is war waged by the weak against the strong.

Much of the fighting during the Revolutionary War (1775–1783) could be called guerrilla warfare. Frontiersment often launched sneak attacks on British forces, who were unprepared for such tactics.

▶ COUNTER-TERRORISM
Armed with Heckler and Koch MP5 sub-machine guns, a counter-terrorist team prepares to board a plane. They wear respirators with darkened eyepieces to protect against exploding stun grenades.

The word "guerrilla" was first applied to fighting during the Peninsular War of 1808–1814, when the Spanish attacked French troops in the mountains of Spain. Their operations were called *guerrilla, or* "a little war."

In 1871 in Paris, following the defeat of the French by the Prussians, the population rose in revolt against the French government. People felt that the government had betrayed them. They formed the Commune, which ruled Paris from March 19, 1871 until May 1871, when it was brutally suppressed by the French Army. The name that

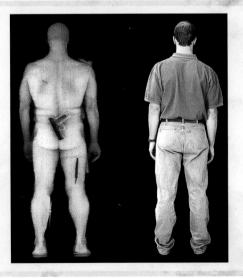

TERRORISM: THE WAR OF THE WEAK

The word "terrorism" dates back to the so-called Reign of Terror which followed the French Revolution in 1789. Between 1793 and 1794 more than 17,000 French citizens were executed, and many more perished in less formal circumstances.

Modern terrorism uses the shock value of an act, such as a random bombing, a hijack, a kidnap, or a shooting, to create a widespread sense of fear and insecurity in the community. The terrorists hope that this fear will eventually affect government policies. Terrorists who overthrow repressive governments can in turn sometimes fail to respect human rights.

The driving force behind a terrorist group may be politics, nationalism, or religion. Terrorist tactics have also been employed by criminal organizations for blackmail, extortion, or punishment.

▶ CONCEALED WEAPONS
Terrorists have devised various ways of carrying handguns, knives, and grenades in places where they will not be detected in quick body searches by police or security forces.

▲ ROBOT AID
Robot-tracked vehicles have been developed to approach, examine, and disrupt terrorist explosive devices. TV cameras mounted on the robot allow the operator to see the device on remotely located monitors, and shotguns or very high-pressure water blast the device apart before it can explode.

the members of the Paris Commune gave themselves — communards—lives on in "communist."

In Russia, from 1917 to 1921, the revolution against the csar (emperor) and his government turned into a civil war. The two opposing sides were the Bolshevik "Reds" and the pro-Western "Whites." The 20th century also saw the growth of guerrilla war, as those countries defeated and occupied by Nazi Germany continued to fight secretly and "resist" their occupiers. The French Resistance, for example, was assisted with weapons and equipment sent from Britain by parachute at night.

Mao Tse-tung led the Chinese Communists against the Japanese in World War II and against the Chinese Nationalists both before and after World War II. Along with Che Guevara, who fought for Castro in Cuba, Mao Tse Tung is one of the most famous writers on the subject of guerrilla warfare.

During the Cold War, the period of tension between the former Soviet Union and the West between the years 1945 and 1989, the Soviet Union supported wars of national liberation or decolonization. In most of these campaigns guerrilla, or terrorist tactics were used. Modern society is very vulnerable to such pinpoint attacks, which can throw ordinary life into chaos. The targets are usually public figures, policemen, or small groups of soldiers, who are ambushed. Public utilities, transportation, and communications can be attacked with explosives. The aim of terrorists is to make a country ungovernable so that the population force its government to strike a deal in order to achieve a peaceful life.

◀ CLIMBER
The rubber tracks on this explosive ordnance device (EOD) vehicle allow it to climb steps and enter buildings where a device may be hidden in a totally inaccessible location.

▼ THE TERRORIST CELL
The cell structure has evolved in terrorist organizations during the 20th century. If contact between large numbers is avoided, it is harder for the security forces to insert their own secret agents into the organizations. If the number of members in contact with each other is kept down to two or three, it is difficult to break up an organization even if some of its members have been arrested.

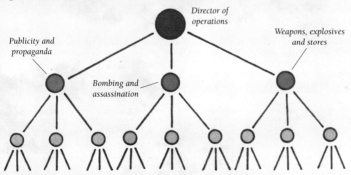

Director of operations

Publicity and propaganda

Bombing and assassination

Weapons, explosives and stores

Key Dates

- 1789 French Revolution begins.
- 1808–1814 Peninsular War.
- 1871 Paris Commune.
- 1917 Russian Revolution.
- 1923–1949 Chinese Revolution.
- 1934– Arab-Israeli conflict .
- 1939–1945 Resistance operations in Nazi-occupied Europe.
- 1945–1962 War in South-east Asia.
- 1949–1962 Algerian War.
- 1945–1975 Indo-China War.
- 1956–1960 Cuban Revolution.
- 1978–1982 Islamic revolution.

Tanks

▲ WORLD WAR I TANK
The Mark I tank could cross a 10-foot trench and had a range of 15 miles.

WHEN THE FIRST TANKS lumbered through the smoke and mud toward German trenches in World War I, the startled Germans thought that they had seen monsters from hell.

The first tank was the idea of Colonel Ernest Swinton in World War I. He took the tracked chassis of the gasoline-driven Holt tractor and combined it with armor plate protection and field-gun or machine-gun armament. These vehicles were called "land ships," but when they were shipped from Britain to France hidden under canvas sheets they were described as "tanks." Curious soldiers were told that they were large water tanks. The name "tank" stuck. Large numbers of these

▶ TIGER TANK
The German Tiger tank weighed 56 tons and was armed with a 3¹/₂ inch gun.

armored tracked vehicles went into action in France, at Cambrai in 1917 and at Amiens in 1918.

In the interwar years tank designs changed. New features included improved suspension and radio communications, and the main armament was mounted in a rotating turret. World War II saw the development of fighting tactics that used the protection, firepower and mobility of tanks to attack and advance quickly, outflanking or encircling a less mobile enemy. Tanks grew in weight and firepower throughout World War II, finishing with the Soviet IS-3 which weighed 44.2 tons and was armed with a 5inch gun.

In the postwar years, changes in tank design included improved engines, suspension, armor, fire control systems, and armament. The American M-60 and the British-designed Centurion saw action in Asia and the Middle East. The Soviet T-54/55 was used throughout the 1950s and 1960s by many countries.

New armor developed in the 1980s includes systems that explode outward if hit by an anti-tank missile and plates of very hard materials that can be bolted on as extra protection. Fire control systems consist of onboard computers which automatically give the correct elevation, the angle of the gun's barrel, and

CLASSIC TANKS

Since 1916 tanks have played a major part in all significant land actions. In World War II some tanks achieved fame because of the quality of their design—for example the Russian T-34 or German Panzer. Others, such as the Sherman, were mass produced, and it was their quantity that caused the greatest impact. However, tank designs since World War II have become increasingly like combat aircraft, with electronics and automation taking over many of the functions that used to be taken on by the crew.

◀ CHALLENGER II
Britain's Challenger tank of the 1980s and 1990s has four crew and weighs 62,000kg.

▶ AMERICAN 1940S SHERMAN
The Sherman weighs 74,400lbs., has a 100-mile range and carries a crew of five.

▲ SWEDISH CV90
This tank weighs 65,000lbs. and has three crew and eight soldiers.

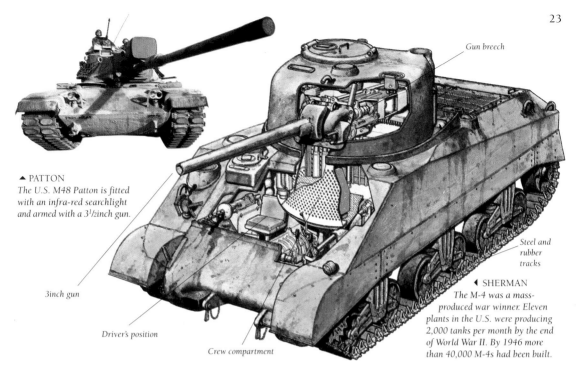

Gun breech

▲ PATTON
*The U.S. M48 Patton is fitted
with an infra-red searchlight
and armed with a 3¹/₂inch gun.*

3inch gun

Driver's position

Crew compartment

Steel and
rubber
tracks

◀ SHERMAN
*The M-4 was a mass-
produced war winner. Eleven
plants in the U.S. were producing
2,000 tanks per month by the end
of World War II. By 1946 more
than 40,000 M-4s had been built.*

ammunition type to the gun once a target has been identified. The fire control is linked with sights that allow the crew to see the heat patterns of enemy vehicles by day and night. The new armament includes guns that fire shells or guided missiles. The new shells are made from very hard materials and are designed to punch through the armor of enemy tanks. One of the most recent major tank actions was fought as part of the Gulf War, between the Coalition Forces and the Iraqis in 1991 following the invasion of Kuwait by Iraq. The new, state-of-the-art technology of the American Abrams and British Challenger tanks gave them the advantage over the older Russian- and Chinese-built T-72 and Type 59 tanks.

▼ TANK TACTICS
Using the terrain, an experienced crew locates the enemy. They can fire at the enemy without exposing themselves. If the main armament can be depressed low enough, the tank can fire from this position. If it drives forward, the gun can still be depressed to point at the enemy tank, but would be more exposed to attack.

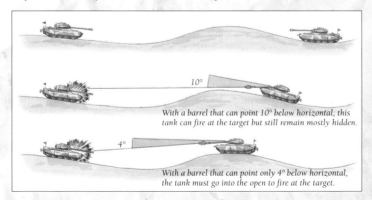

10°

*With a barrel that can point 10° below horizontal, this
tank can fire at the target but still remain mostly hidden.*

4°

*With a barrel that can point only 4° below horizontal,
the tank must go into the open to fire at the target.*

Key Dates

- 1916 September: first tanks used in World War I.

- 1943 July–September: Battle of Kursk—2,700 German tanks against 3,300 Soviet tanks.

- 1945 August: invasion of Manchuria—5,500 Soviet tanks attack 1,000 Japanese tanks.

- 1967 Middle East War—1,000 Israeli tanks vs. 2,050 Egyptian, Syrian, and Jordanian tanks.

- 1973 Middle East War—2,000 Israeli tanks vs. 4,800 Egyptian, Syrian, Jordanian, and Iraqi tanks.

- 1991 Gulf War—2,200 Coalition tanks vs. 4,000 Iraqi tanks.

Anti-Tank Weapons

A NTI-TANK GUNNERS need to have the cool nerve of an old-style big-game hunter. As the enemy tank crashes toward them, perhaps firing its machine guns, the anti-tank crew must wait until their enemy is in range and then fire at its most vulnerable point.

As soon as tanks had appeared on the Western Front in World War I, all the combatants began to think of ways of stopping or destroying these machines by using anti-tank weapons.

The Imperial German Army developed a powerful bolt-action anti-tank rifle firing a .50in bullet. Most armies, however, relied on the crews of field guns to shoot it out with these early tanks. Anti-tank rifles were used by the British and Soviet armies in the opening years of World War II, but thicker armor and new weapons soon made them obsolete.

The true anti-tank gun, which was developed in the 1920s and 1930s, fired a very hard shell at high velocity. Early guns were between 1½inch and 2¼inch in caliber. As World War II progressed the guns grew bigger, and the Germans used the 3½inch antiaircraft gun as a very effective anti-tank gun. The Russians used a huge 4inch gun.

The major change in anti-tank weapons came with the development of the shaped charge and short-range rockets. The shaped charge penetrated all conventional armor, while there was no recoil with a rocket projectile. The weapon that combined rocket and shaped charge was the American 2⅓inch rocket launcher M1. It was nicknamed the "Bazooka" after the musical instrument played by the U.S. comedian Bob Burns.

▲ EXPLOSION
A Swedish BILL anti-tank missile explodes above the turret of a target tank.

▲ INFANTRY ANTI-TANK
Anti-tank weapons may have a crew, for example the M40 4¼inch recoilless rifle or the TOW or Milan missiles, or they may be single-shot one-man weapons such as the M72 or the RPG-7.

PENETRATION

Most infantry anti-tank weapons have a shaped charge warhead. This consists of explosives shaped around the outside of a copper cone. When the warhead explodes, the energy of the explosion is pushed inward and forward, creating a jet of molten metal and gas. A slug of metal at the front then melts its way through the armor of the tank.

◀ CARL GUSTAV
Canadian soldiers use the Swedish 3½inch recoilless anti-tank weapon called the Carl Gustav. It can fire a wide range of ammunition.

▲ BILL
The launcher of the revolutionary Swedish BILL missile is fitted with a thermal imaging (TI) sight. It can detect the heat generated by the engine of a tank or fighting vehicle and use it as a target. This technology can also be used just as a night-vision device by troops on reconnaissance missions during darkness.

▶ FAIRCHILD A-10
The Fairchild A-10A has the official title Thunderbolt II, but is known as "the Warthog" by its crews. It has a powerful multi-barrel 1¹/₅inch GAU-8 cannon in the nose and can also carry anti-tank missiles and bombs.

At the close of the war the Germans had looked at the concept of an anti-tank guided weapon (ATGW), which they designated the X-7. It had a range of 3,280 feet, weighed 25lbs. and would be guided to its target by signals passed along a light wire that was on a spool on the launching mount. The X-7 was reported to be capable of penetrating 8 inches of armor.

Most modern ATGWs are wire guided because this is a reliable system that cannot be jammed by the enemy. Warhead design has changed as armor has improved, and now consists of two or even three shaped charges that detonate in succession. In 1979 Sweden produced a missile designated BILL, which explodes above the tank, sending its shaped charge jet through the thin top armor. These two designs, called "tandem warheads" and "top attack," indicate the direction that anti-tank weapon technology will take in the 21st century.

◀ TANK DESTROYER
A British Alvis Striker firing a wire-guided Swingfire anti-tank missile. The Swingfire has a maximum range of 13,120 feet.

▼ LAW
The M72 LAW is a telescopic rocket launcher that weighs 8¹/₂lbs. It has an effective range of 722 feet. It was first used in action in the Vietnam War, and later by the British in the Falklands in 1982.

▼ DESTRUCTION
An Iraqi tank destroyed by American A-10s during the Gulf War. The tank has almost blown apart, because the ammunition and fuel inside have exploded. Internal explosions are a constant worry for all armored vehicle crews.

Key Dates

- 1918 German .5 inch anti-tank rifles in use.
- 1927 First dedicated anti-tank guns developed.
- 1942 "Bazooka" rocket launcher developed in U.S.
- 1943 German PaK 43/41 anti-tank gun enters service.
- 1956 French introduce Nord SS10 wire-guided missile.
- 1972 Euromissile Milan produced.
- 1973 Egyptians use Sagger guided missiles in Sinai.
- 1979 Swedish BILL developed.

Transportation

▲ AIRBORNE
A rocket-armed Blackhawk helicopter carries a two-man reconnaissance vehicle as an underslung load.

When armies go to war they use forms of transportation similar to those used by ordinary people—car, train, ship, and plane. For centuries they relied on human or animal power for transportation. Oxen, horses, and mules pulled wagons and guns; and troops carried heavy loads in packs.

Ships were vital for island nations such as Britain because they could transport troops overseas and, if necessary, evacuate them. In World War II amphibious operations became highly specialized, with landing craft designed to put troops and vehicles ashore on open beaches.

The steam locomotive made troop transportation faster and allowed large numbers of troops and equipment to be moved around. The Civil War (1861–1865) demonstrated the importance of a reliable railroad system. Railroad lines, and particularly, bridges became a key target for raids by troops and, later on, by aircraft.

At the beginning of World War I vehicles such as taxis and buses were used to move troops quickly. Later, trucks became more readily available. Huge numbers of trucks were used in World War II, increasing the need for fuel supplies. After D-Day, in June 1944, a fuel pipeline was laid from Britain to northern France across the Channel. It was codenamed PLUTO, which stands for Pipe Line Under The Ocean.

Among the wheeled vehicles produced in World War II the ¼-ton Jeep remains the

◀ MOTORBIKE
A German Afrika Korps BMW R75 motorcycle combination, armed with an MG34 machine gun, roars through the Libyan desert in 1942.

AMPHIBIOUS OPERATIONS
World War II saw the development of specialized landing craft to carry vehicles, troops, and stores for amphibious operations. Before 1942 soldiers went ashore from small boats, ships, or modified freighters. In the Pacific, the U.S. Marine Corps used tracked amphibious APCs to carry marines ashore.

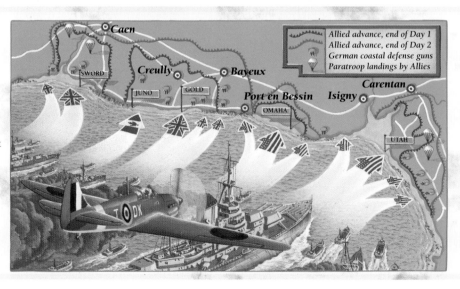

Allied advance, end of Day 1
Allied advance, end of Day 2
German coastal defense guns
Paratroop landings by Allies

Caen
SWORD
Creully
JUNO
GOLD
Bayeux
Port en Bessin
OMAHA
Isigny
Carentan
UTAH

◀ EXTRA ARMOR
An Israeli M113 APC, in desert camouflage, is fitted with extra armor and carries a .50in Browning machine gun. APCs have enough internal space to make them ideal weapons carriers for missiles, AA guns, or spare ammunition. They are also used as ambulances and for radio communications.

▼ HUMVEE FIREPOWER
A TOW anti-tank missile streaks away from its launcher, which is mounted on an HMMWV, a wheeled utility vehicle known to U.S. soldiers as a "HumVee." The rugged and reliable HumVee is popular with U.S. service personnel because it is easy to drive.

most enduring symbol. The U.S. produced 639,245 Jeeps before the war ended, and the Jeep continued to serve in many armies into the 1960s. In World War II the U.S.-designed DUKW, a six-wheeled amphibious truck, was used during amphibious operations to ferry stores from ships to the shore. Despite their age, DUKWs were still being used by the British Royal Marines in the late 1990s.

Most armies now use 4-ton trucks and light ³/₄-ton vehicles. However, some specialized Alpine regiments still use mules to carry heavy equipment such as mortars, pack howitzers, and ammunition up narrow mountain tracks.

◀ D-DAY LANDINGS
Landings at beaches in Normandy, codenamed Utah, Omaha, Gold, Juno, and Sword, began at 6.30 a.m. on June 6, 1944. By midnight 57,000 U.S. and 75,000 British and Canadian troops and their equipment were ashore.

▲ LANDING CRAFT
U.S. soldiers approach Omaha Beach in Normandy in June 1944. They are in a Higgins boat, a landing craft designed to carry soldiers.

◀ DUCK
The DUKW, a wartime amphibious truck, was nicknamed the "DUCK." It is still in service with the Royal Marines in Britain.

Key Dates

- 1885 Four-wheel motor carriage developed.
- 1914 French use 600 taxis to transport troops at the Marne.
- 1925 French demonstrate the half-track vehicle.
- 1927 British Army tests mechanized warfare tactics.
- 1940 Germans conduct trials for an amphibious invasion of Great Britain.
- 1943 U.S. DUKW used in combat.
- 1944 D-Day, the largest amphibious operation in history, takes place in northern France.

Reconnaissance

IMAGINE PLAYING CHESS or another tactical board game, but seeing the board only occasionally or being told about its layout by someone else. You would be "in the dark." A chess player wants to see how the game is developing, perhaps look at the opponent's expression, and make moves based on this information.

In war, reconnaissance is somewhat like watching the board and the player. It is the tactical method of learning about enemy positions, movements, or plans and finding out about the terrain or weather in which combat may take place.

For many centuries the job of reconnaissance was done by small patrols of light cavalry riding ahead of the main body of troops. The only special equipment available was a telescope or a pair of binoculars. If they

▲ SAS JEEP
A U.S.-made Jeep fitted with Vickers K machine guns in service with the SAS in North Africa.

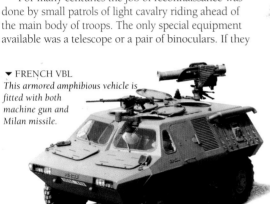

▼ FRENCH VBL
This armored amphibious vehicle is fitted with both machine gun and Milan missile.

saw the enemy, they would then ride as fast as possible to pass the information back.

The pedal bicycle was popular at the turn of the 19th century because cyclist troops were fast, silent, and very mobile. However, reconnaisance changed dramatically with the development of the internal combustion engine and of small, reliable radios.

Armored cars and motorcycles had been developed in World War I. Between 1939 and 1943 German soldiers used them most effectively and set the style for armored reconnaissance. Pushing ahead, they would find undefended bridges, gaps in minefields, and weak points

MODERN VISION
Reconnaissance by land, sea, and air uses a huge range of sensors to gather information about the enemy and its plans and forces. Once this information has been collected, the most important step is to put it all together and assess its value. This assessment must then be passed as quickly as possible to the commanders and units so that they can make best use of it.

▶ PHOTOGRAPHY
Photographs are useful because they can be processed quickly and are easy to handle. Extra information can be overprinted on them, combining the accuracy of a photo with the information found on a map.

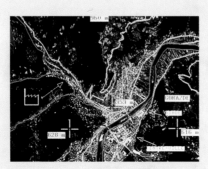

▲ DRONE LAUNCH
A remotely piloted vehicle (RPV) is also known as a drone. It is a small aircraft fitted with cameras and sensors. Drones are designed to be flown by remote control over enemy territory.

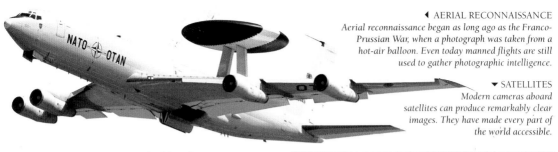

Aerial reconnaissance began as long ago as the Franco-Prussian War, when a photograph was taken from a hot-air balloon. Even today manned flights are still used to gather photographic intelligence.

▼ SATELLITES
Modern cameras aboard satellites can produce remarkably clear images. They have made every part of the world accessible.

in defended positions. This valuable information would be quickly radioed back, and the main forces would follow up.

Reconnaissance could also be undertaken by foot patrols working away from their vehicles, and even by scuba divers and midget submarines. In the months before D-Day, in 1944, the beaches of northern France were visited by small groups of divers. They swam ashore to check the gradient of each beach and its defenses, and to discover whether it was sand, shingle, or mud, as this was important for the landing troops.

In the war in the Falklands in 1982, men of the Special Boat Service (SBS) and the Special Air Service (SAS) landed on the islands to observe Argentinian positions. They helped the planners to build up a picture of the strength and quality of the garrison. In the 1990–1991 Gulf War, the British SAS entered Iraq to report on the terrain. It was what they hoped for: a gravel desert which was better for the tanks and armored vehicles.

Reconnaissance intelligence is also gathered from aerial photographs and radar images taken by special

reconnaissance aircraft. The most recent technique for gathering reconnaissance intelligence is by remotely piloted vehicles (RPVs). They are usually small aircraft fitted with cameras that transmit TV images of the terrain to the base from which the RPV is being operated. They give information about enemy movements and positions.

▼ DRONE FLIGHT
Modern drones send back "real-time" TV and sensor information as they fly a search pattern over a designated area. If the operator "sees" something of interest, the drone can fly lower or use more powerful sensors.

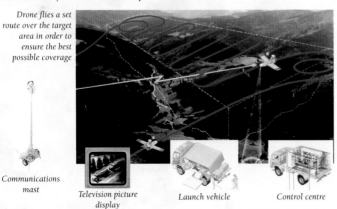

Drone flies a set route over the target area in order to ensure the best possible coverage

Communications mast

Television picture display

Launch vehicle

Control centre

Key Dates

- 1858 First aerial photography.
- 1866 Typewriter invented.
- 1888 First portable roll-film camera.
- 1923 Cathode-ray tube, used in televisions, invented.
- 1943 Infrared night-vision viewer used.
- 1957 First space satellite launched.
- 1960 U-2 reconnaissance aircraft flown by Gary Powers shot down over the former Soviet Union.
- 1982 SAS and SBS forces used for reconnaissance in the Falklands.

Communications

▲ CARRIER PIGEON
A homing pigeon carries simple messages in a capsule attached to its leg.

I N A FAST-MOVING GAME such as a football match, information can mean the difference between victory or defeat, communicating tactics and positions. In wartime, this kind of communication is even more critical—the lives of thousands of soldiers are at risk. Ships, aircraft, and many other military units report their positions, which allows a commander to build up a picture of the battle.

For centuries messages were sent either verbally or as a written dispatch and carried by foot or horseback. Beacons positioned on high hills were lit if there was a threat of enemy invasion or attack. Signal flags used at sea were a key to the British victory at Trafalgar on October 21, 1805. In 19th-century India and South Africa, where the air was clear and the sunshine constant, devices called heliographs used reflective mirrors to flash Morse code signals.

The Morse code could also be used with signal lamps; this method of communication was particularly effective at sea. The telegraph, which allowed Morse messages to be sent over long distances, was first used in the Civil War (1861–1865).

▲ FIELD RADIO
A modern field radio is light and reliable. It may even have a built-in security system which makes it impossible to decode a message without the correct equipment.

CODES AND SIGNALS

Signaling systems were initially visual ones, using flags, light, or even smoke. They allowed people to communicate beyond the range of the human voice. Telegraph, telephone, and radio increased the range. However, the danger of interception by the enemy made it essential that signals be in code.

A	● ■	J	● ■ ■ ■	S	● ● ●
B	■ ● ● ●	K	■ ● ■	T	■
C	■ ● ■ ●	L	● ■ ● ●	U	● ● ■
D	■ ● ●	M	■ ■	V	● ● ● ■
E	●	N	■ ●	W	● ■ ■
F	● ● ■ ●	O	■ ■ ■	X	■ ● ● ■
G	■ ■ ●	P	● ■ ■ ●	Y	■ ● ■ ■
H	● ● ● ●	Q	■ ■ ● ■	Z	■ ■ ● ●
I	● ●	R	● ■ ●		

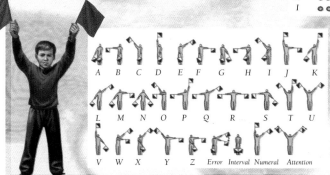

A B C D E F G H I J K
L M N O P Q R S T U
V W X Y Z Error Interval Numeral Attention

◀ SEMAPHORE
The British Army and the Royal Navy used this signaling system before radio was developed. The advantage of semaphore is that flags don't operate from an electronic system, which can break down.

▲ MORSE CODE
Invented by Samuel Morse in 1850, this "dot and dash" code was the key to the telegraph system. It was first used operationally during the Crimean War.

◀ WARTIME RADIO
French troops with American uniforms and equipment operate a radio during fighting in Germany in 1945.

▶ CONCEALED
Men of the U.S. Army's 82nd Airborne Division during the invasion of Grenada in 1983. The soldier carries the radio in a medium pack to conceal it.

The telephone was in widespread use by 1880 and was used in the Boer War (1899–1902) and the Russo-Japanese War (1904–1905). In World War I, field telephones were developed, and telephone cables were laid quickly to connect headquarters with the artillery batteries.

The first radios were cumbersome and required a wagon and team of horses to transport them. In 1915, an observer used a radio in a hot-air balloon over the Dardanelles in Turkey. During the interwar years radios became small enough to fit in a backpack.

Most military radios operate in the very high frequency (VHF) range between 30 and 200 megahertz (MHz) and in the high frequency (HF) range between 1 and 30MHz. Anyone with a radio receiver tuned to the right frequency could listen to a radio conversation, and so codes were introduced. However, even if a message

was encoded, the station could be jammed by a powerful signal. One technique for ensuring security and avoiding jamming was "burst transmission." A message would be prepared and then sent in a few seconds to another station which would display it on a screen. In the 1980s radios were designed that could change frequencies at random intervals. If the receiving station was correctly tuned it would follow the "hops," and so a conversation could take place without interruption.

The latest development in radio communications are satellites. They receive radio signals and rebroadcast them, allowing messages from remote locations to be transmitted reliably over huge distances.

▲ SUNLIGHT
A British soldier uses a signaling mirror to contact a circling helicopter. It is a silent but effective communications tool.

▶ THE ENIGMA CODE
During World War II the Germans used a variety of codes. Most of them used a machine to jumble up the letters of the message. The British, assisted by the French, Poles, and Americans, were able to break the German codes. This literally saved Britain from starvation because some of these codes were for the U-boats, which were sinking ships carrying food and fuel to Britain. The code machines were like very complex typewriters.

Key Dates

- 1850 Morse Code invented.
- 1858 Heliograph invented.
- 1876 Telephone invented.
- 1892 First detected radio signal.
- 1901 Transatlantic radio link established.
- 1921 Teleprinter developed.
- 1925 Shortwave, crystal-controlled radio invented.
- 1926 Enigma coding machine developed.
- 1949 Transistor invented.
- 1960 Microchip first used.

Protecting the Soldier

▲ THE HELMET
The helmet, such as this M1 steel helmet, is the oldest and most effective protection for a soldier.

ARMOR HAD PROTECTED soldiers when firearms were awkward and heavy and the sword was still used in warfare. However, armor was no longer worn once firearms improved and freedom of movement had become more important.

Like the "hard hats" worn by construction workers on building sites, the steel helmets introduced in World War I were intended to protect soldiers from objects falling on their heads. Such objects are normally shrapnel, the tiny fragments that fall from the sky when a shell explodes. During World War I armored protection was introduced for snipers—soldiers who use powerful rifles with telescopic sights to shoot at an unwary enemy or important targets such as officers. This protection was very unwieldy and heavy, and resembled the breastplates of medieval soldiers.

Following the use of poison gas by the Germans on the Western Front in World War I, gas masks or respirators were produced. The first masks were simply cotton pads worn with goggles, but by the end of the war respirators were not only more effective but also more comfortable to wear. Modern masks use charcoal filters. Charcoal is a very useful filter against impurities, hence its use in domestic water filters. It is also used in soldiers' protective jackets and trousers.

▲ REACTIVE ARMOR
Explosive reactive armor (ERA) comes in bolt-on slabs. It explodes outward when hit, counteracting the penetration of charges.

PROTECT AND SURVIVE

As weapons became more effective and more lethal, soldiers looked for ways of improving their protection. Soldiers who were fighting a defensive battle dug themselves in, and built log or sandbag defenses or, even better, reinforced concrete ones. The difficulties came when they were in the open. Thick steel plates gave protection, but their weight meant that soldiers could move only short distances at low speed.

In the 1980s and 1990s new materials have allowed soldiers to move freely with protection from shell fragments and bullets. Fireproof materials, used in tank and aircraft crew overalls, protect the wearer against flash burns from exploding fuel tanks. In bad weather troops now have the comfort of breathable raincoats.

British helmet, World War I

British paratrooper's helmet, 1944

British helmet no. 4, 1944

U.S. M1 steel helmet, World War II

Current British no. 6 helmet

Current U.S. PASGT Kevlar helmet

◀ EVACUATION OF
CASUALTIES
*U.S. soldiers carry a casualty
on a litter to a Blackhawk
helicopter. Helicopters were
first used for flying wounded
from the battlefield during the
Korean War and have become
a vital link in the casualty
evacuation chain. Nicknamed
"Dust Off" in the Vietnam War,
helicopters could literally take
an injured man from deep in
the jungle and fly him to a
modern hospital. He could be
admitted to a fully equipped
operating room in less than an
hour. Many troops who would
have died in earlier times
because of a lack of prompt
and thorough medical support
now survive terrible battlefield
injuries.*

In World War II protective jackets with overlapping steel plates were produced to protect American bomber crews from the shrapnel from German antiaircraft (flak) guns. The jackets were called "flak jackets."

Today's body armor is made from materials such as Kevlar, which is light and strong. Its woven form is used for jackets and even boots; it can also be bonded into a plastic for used in helmets. These new materials can protect a soldier, even at close range, from shots from handguns and even rifles.

In the confined spaces of aircraft, warships, and armored vehicles, fire has always been a major threat. In World War II, leather jackets and gloves, as well as goggles, provided some protection. The crews on warships wore steel helmets and anti-flash hoods made from an asbestos-based fabric.

The development of artificial fire-resistant fabrics such as Nomex has allowed gloves, flying overalls, jackets, and trousers to be made from a material with a high level of protection. Tanks and aircraft now have fire detection systems that operate instantly, swamping potential fires with a gas that cuts off the oxygen.

▶ ANGLE OF ARMOR
If the armor on an armored fighting vehicle is sloped, this increases the distance through which a projectile has to pass before it breaks through to the interior. If a projectile strikes the armor at an oblique angle it may even ricochet and fall away harmlessly.

Armour that is 8mm thick when vertical, is 11mm thick when tilted

Key Dates

- 1856 Bessemer steel produced.
- 1865 First antiseptics used.
- 1882 Armored steel developed.
- 1914–1918 World War I: steel helmets introduced to protect soldiers from shrapnel.
- 1920s Gas masks and respirators introduced after the use of poison gas in World War I.
- 1939–1945 World War II: penicillin, plastic surgery, and blood transfusions introduced.
- 1970s Explosive reactive armor, ceramic armor, Kevlar, and Nomex developed.

▲ ARMORED TRAIN
A Soviet armored train captured by the Germans in World War II. Armor protected the crew, but the train was vulnerable if the tracks were destroyed or damaged.

Armored Vehicles

▲ ARMORED CAR
The first armored car, the Charron Girardot et Voigt, was built in France in 1904.

As far back as 1482 the idea of an armored fighting vehicle (AFV) appeared in sketches drawn by Leonardo da Vinci. It was propelled by muscle power, with the crew operating geared hand cranks and firing muskets through slits. However, it was the British War Office that saw the first true AFV in 1902 when the Simms "War Car" was demonstrated. It used a gasoline engine to drive a wheeled vehicle at a maximum speed of 11mph. It was protected by ¼ inch of armor and armed with two machine guns and a one-pounder gun.

The Belgians and British Royal Navy used armored cars with machine guns in 1914. However, the mud of the Western Front was unsuitable for wheeled vehicles. Armored cars were used in the Middle East by the British when fighting against the Turks.

The interwar period saw the development of six- and even eight-wheeled armored cars and the half-track. This vehicle had tracks at the rear of its chassis and wheels at the front. It had the cross-country performance of a tank but could be driven like a truck. The German Sdkfz 251 and American M3 half-track were widely used in World War II.

◀ ARMORED PERSONNEL CARRIER (APC)
This M113 APC is fitted with TOW anti-tank missile launchers. APCs are used in both wartime conflicts and civil disturbances.

PROTECTION AND MOBILITY

Armor protection is used for combat vehicles and also to protect VIP (Very Important Person) cars and vehicles used by the media in hostile locations. Protection may be quite basic, consisting of plates and panels, or it may be a system that is both bulletproof and mineproof.

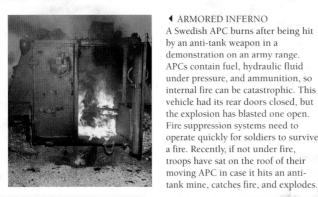

◀ ARMORED INFERNO
A Swedish APC burns after being hit by an anti-tank weapon in a demonstration on an army range. APCs contain fuel, hydraulic fluid under pressure, and ammunition, so internal fire can be catastrophic. This vehicle had its rear doors closed, but the explosion has blasted one open. Fire suppression systems need to operate quickly for soldiers to survive a fire. Recently, if not under fire, troops have sat on the roof of their moving APC in case it hits an anti-tank mine, catches fire, and explodes.

▲ BRITISH SAXON APC
The 4 x 4 Saxon is effectively an armoured truck. It weighs 24,850lbs., can carry 10 soldiers and has a top speed on roads of 60mph. It has been used in Northern Ireland and Bosnia to transport troops under armor.

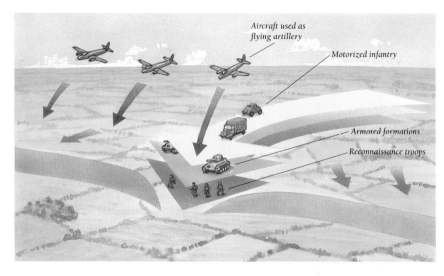

◄ ARMORED ATTACK
The armored tactics pioneered by the Germans in 1939–1942 used aircraft as flying artillery. At the front were reconnaissance troops, followed by armored formations and backed by motorized infantry in trucks. The tanks were massed to punch through enemy defenses. The infantry secured the flanks as the armored troops plunged deeper into enemy territory.

Aircraft used as flying artillery

Motorized infantry

Armored formations

Reconnaissance troops

After the war the M3 was used by the Israeli Army up to 1967. The half-track also allowed infantry to keep pace with fast-moving tanks. Artillery mounted on tracked chassis could bombard enemy positions before the infantry and tanks attacked.

Before D-Day, on June 6, 1944, the British developed several special tanks, nicknamed "Funnies." They included tanks that could clear paths through minefields, lay special matting roads across shingle beaches, or lay bridges over ditches. Another of these special tanks was the Armored Vehicle Royal Engineers (AVRE) which could fire a 45lb. demolition bomb 690 feet against German fortifications. The armored engineer vehicle that can lay bridges or bulldoze rubble is now a standard vehicle in most major armies.

Since the end of World War II, AFVs have been developed as armored ambulances, recovery vehicles, mobile workshops, headquarters, nuclear biological and chemical (NBC) detection vehicles, and troop carriers. They are wheeled like the French VAB or fully tracked like the American M113. The wheeled APCs are widely used in United Nation peacekeeping operations because they give protection against rifle and machine gun fire as well as from shell fragments.

▲ FRENCH PANHARD ERC
Armed with a 3½ inch gun, the French ERC Sagaie armored car has a top speed of 60mph on roads. Its six wheels give it a better cross-country performance than a normal four-wheeled vehicle. The ERC saw action during the Gulf War of 1990–1991 against Iraq.

Key Dates

- 1904 First armored car.
- 1914 Armored car shoots down German Taube aircraft.
- 1919–1922 Armored cars used in Ireland against the IRA.
- 1920 Rolls Royce armored car introduced; it serves until 1941.
- 1931 First cast turrets introduced by France for the D1.
- 1932 Japanese field the first diesel-powered armored vehicle.
- 1936 Torsion bar suspension introduced by the Germans.
- 1944 Tetrach light tanks land by glider in Normandy, France.

Camouflage

EXAMPLES OF CAMOUFLAGE exist all around us in nature. Birds, fish, and other animals have self-protection in the form of colors that help them blend into the background of vegetation, sky, water, or sand.

The earliest military camouflage consisted of the dark-green tunics and black buttons adopted by the British rifle regiments during the Peninsular War of 1808–1814. The British had learned camouflage and field craft from the experience of fighting the American Colonists and Native Americans in North America in the late 18th century. The red coats of the British stood out clearly in battle, making them easy targets.

In India in the 1800s, British troops dyed their white tropical uniforms with tea to produce a shade of brown that Indians called *khak*, or dust colored. These "khaki" uniforms helped the troops to blend into the dry terrain as they fought against tribes on the Northwest Frontier.

In World War I camouflage, a word taken from the French *camouflet* meaning "smoke puff," became a serious technique. The French Army used conscripted artists to devise color schemes to conceal artillery and vehicles. Some were in fantastic shapes and colors, and also included nets with strips of colored cloth that were draped over buildings, guns, and vehicles.

▲ GREEN AND BROWN
A British soldier in the black, green, brown, and buff camouflage that was introduced in the early 1970s. It is designed to mimic the shadows and highlights of natural vegetation. It is effective in tropical and temperate terrain and has been adopted by the Dutch and Indonesian armies.

▲ DESERT
A soldier in the desert with his helmet garnished with nylon "scrim" to break up its outline. His equipment and clothing have softened with use and do not present hard, unnatural lines and shapes.

MEN AND MACHINES

Camouflage conceals soldiers, vehicles, and buildings. It may consist of paint patterns, netting, painted screens, planted vegetation, or even fake buildings and vehicles. Good camouflage fools the naked eye, but special photographic film and night-vision equipment will penetrate ordinary camouflage. Special nets and paints have, in turn, been developed to counter this technology.

▶ FACE PAINT
A soldier with some of the elaborate patterns that can be painted to break up the shape and color of the human face. Grass has been added to his helmet.

▲ HELMET COVERS
U.S. military helmets with cotton drill desert camouflage covers. This spotted pattern is known to U.S. service personnel as "chocolate chip cookie" camouflage. The elastic band around the helmet is used to secure vegetation for camouflage.

▲ SNOW
In the course of an exercise in the 1980s in northern Canada, Canadian Army Special Forces slog through the snow in white camouflaged uniforms and backpack covers. They have fixed white tape to their weapons to break up the outline.

▼ SLOGGING
U.S. soldiers armed with M16 rifles and carrying knapsacks slog through the dust. They are wearing camouflaged uniforms. Their Kevlar helmets have cloth covers made from the same material.

The development of aircraft and aerial photography during the two world wars made camouflage essential. Elaborate deception schemes included building fake vehicles and constructing huts with lighting that operated by itself at night.

By the end of the 20th century new methods of detection had taken camouflage out of the simple visual detection range. These methods included night-vision equipment and thermal imaging, enabling the viewer to see the heat generated by humans or equipment. Modern camouflage can conceal the shape, color, heat, and radar picture of aircraft, ships, and tanks.

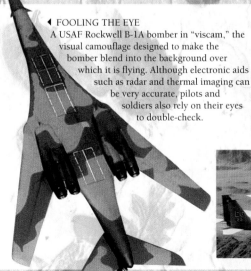

◀ FOOLING THE EYE
A USAF Rockwell B-1A bomber in "viscam," the visual camouflage designed to make the bomber blend into the background over which it is flying. Although electronic aids such as radar and thermal imaging can be very accurate, pilots and soldiers also rely on their eyes to double-check.

▼ JETS OVER THE DESERT
Two F-15 Eagles are in flight with a chase plane over the desert. The Eagles are painted in pale "air superiority" camouflage which is designed to blend into the sky.

Key Dates

- 1775–1783 American Revolution: use of field craft by Colonists.

- 1808–1814 Peninsular War: the British riflemen wear dark-green camouflaged tunics.

- 1857–1858 Indian Mutiny: white uniforms dyed "khaki".

- 1914–1918 World War I: land, sea and air camouflage developed.

- 1939–1945 World War II: aerial photography and infrared technology developed.

- 1970s Black, green, brown, and buff camouflage introduced.

Battleships

▲ NELSON
Nelson was one of the greatest naval commanders. One of the secrets of his victories was an efficient flag signaling system.

A CAPITAL SHIP IS A major naval warship. Today's capital ship is probably a submerged submarine with nuclear missiles aboard, or an aircraft carrier. Yet for centuries the capital ship was a battleship such as H.M.S. *Victory*, which was powered by sail and armed with cannons along its hull.

Sea war in the 18th and 19th centuries was a test of sailing skills, stamina, and courage. The gunners learned to load and "run out" the cannons and fire them as quickly as possible to ensure that there was a steady barrage against enemy warships. The wooden-hulled ships were very strong, and when soaked with salty seawater they did not burn easily.

The change came in the mid-19th century with the development of steam propulsion, armor plating, and breech-loading guns. In 1859 the French launched the first steam-powered ironclad battleship, *La Gloire*. It was armed with 36 6½inch guns. Within two years the British had launched the *Warrior*, an ironclad ship with superior protection and armaments.

During the Civil War the indecisive battle between the ironclad battleships *Merrimack* (renamed *Virginia*) and *Monitor* in 1862 gave some clue about the likely outcome of future naval battles.

The battle of Tsu Shima (Toshima) on May 27and 28, 1905, pitted Russian battleships against Japanese ones. The battle ended with a decisive victory for the Japanese naval forces. The Russian defeat at Tsu Shima led ultimately to defeat for the Russian forces in the Russo-Japanese War.

◀ ABOARD THE *MONITOR*
The battle of Hampton Roads, Virginia, on March 8–9, 1862, saw the Confederate armored steam frigate *Merrimack* fight an inconclusive battle with the U.S.S. *Monitor*. The *Monitor* had 11inch guns in a revolving turret.

Muzzle

▶ U.S. CANNON
This 19th-century muzzle-loading ship's cannon has simple gearing on its wooden carriage, which allows the muzzle to be lowered or raised.

FROM WOOD TO IRON
Steam power and armor plate made the new ironclad warships "wolves among a flock of sheep" when they first appeared in a world dominated by wooden sailing ships. An "arms race" developed, with new and more sophisticated ironclad ships being built throughout Europe in the 19th century.

Breech loading

Muzzle

◀ A U.S. 8IN GUN
This gun could be used aboard capital ships or for coastal defense. It is breech loading and is mounted on a turntable trackway to allow it to rotate fully through 360 degrees.

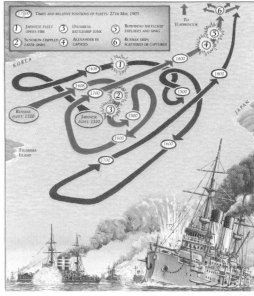

▼ BATTLE OF TRAFALGAR
The Battle of Trafalgar was fought on October 21, 1805, off the Spanish coast. It involved 27 British and 33 French and Spanish ships. The battle was a victory for the British under Nelson.

▲ BATTLE OF TSU SHIMA
This battle between the Imperial Russian Baltic fleet and the Imperial Japanese fleet took place off Korea between May 27 and 28, 1905.

At the beginning of the 20th century the launch of H.M.S. *Dreadnought* in 1906 marked another change in the design of capital ships. It was armed with 10 12inch guns and 27 12-pounder guns. By this time battleships had a speed of 18 knots and weighed 15,000 tonnes.

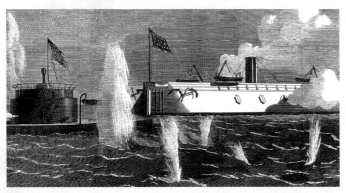

▲ SEA BATTLE
In a sea battle in 1862, during the Civil War, the *Merrimack* (*Virginia*)(*right*) fights it out with the U.S.S. *Monitor*. This battle, which lasted more than four hours, saw the first operational use of armored steam-powered craft in war.

Key Dates

- 1805 October 21: Battle of Trafalgar.
- 1859: French launch the first steam-powered, ironclad battleship, *La Gloire*.
- 1862 March 8–9: Battle of Hampton Roads.
- 1864 August 5: Battle of Mobile Bay.
- 1866 July 20: Battle of Lissa.
- 1898 May 1: Battle of Manila Bay.
- 1905 May 27–28: Battle of Tsu Shima.
- 1906: Launch of HMS *Dreadnought*.

20th-Century Battleships

▲ NIGHT SALVO
A U.S. battleship fires a battery salvo at night.

THE BATTLE OF JUTLAND (1916), in World War I was fought between the capital ships of the British Royal Navy and the Imperial German Navy. The outcome was indecisive.

In the interwar years several countries attempted to reduce the weight of capital ships and the size of their fleets. However, both the Japanese and the Germans were building warships in secret, and they entered World War II with powerful modern ships. The Germans saw their ships as a powerful weapon to attack Allied merchant shipping. As a result, German warships, such as the 49,360-ton battleship *Bismarck,* became a priority target for the Royal Navy. The *Bismarck* was sunk on May 27, 1941, after being pounded by the guns of the battleships H.M.S. *King George V* and H.M.S. *Rodney.*

The development of aircraft carriers and submarines made capital ships very vulnerable. The Japanese battleships *Yamato* and *Mushashi*, the largest and most heavily protected ships of their class in the world, displaced 64,170 tons each. They were armed with nine 18inch guns and twelve 6inch guns. They

had crews of 2,500 men and carried six spotter aircraft. The *Yamato* and the *Mushashi* were sunk by torpedo and dive-bomber aircraft from U.S. carriers on April 7, 1945 and October 24, 1945 respectively. Earlier, H.M.S. *Prince of Wales*, which had fought against the *Bismarck*, was sunk by Japanese aircraft on December 10, 1941.

Battleships fired huge shells, which were very effective in the bombardment of coastal defenses before an amphibious landing. During World War II battleships were used on D-Day and to support the U.S. Marine Corps landings throughout the Pacific.

Today the title of "capital ships" has passed to aircraft carriers and nuclear submarines armed with

▶ CLOSE IN SUPPORT
This U.S. Navy 20mm Phalanx system is radar controlled. The gun fires at 1,000–3,000rpm. Its very hard depleted-uranium rounds are designed to destroy surface-skimming anti-ship missiles such as the Exocet. The Phalanx has a maximum range of 19,680 feet. It can rotate through 100 degrees in one second, and elevate up to 68 degrees in one second. The gun has a 989-round ammunition drum which can be reloaded in 10–30 minutes.

CAPITAL SHIPS

Capital ships, the big warships around which naval fleets are formed, were originally big-gun battleships. Today's surface fleets and task forces are based around the aircraft carrier. Carriers and submarines are nuclear powered, which gives them the ability to stay at sea almost indefinitely and to travel huge distances.

▶ PRESTIGE
Capital ships were the centerpieces of the great navies of the 20th century. In peacetime these great ships would travel the world "showing the flag," visiting the ports of other nations whom their government wished to impress. In wartime, capital ships were the flagships for the admirals in command of battle fleets.

▲ DRESSED OVERALL ▼
These armored, steam-powered warships are "dressed overall" with signal flags displayed as decoration. Modern warships have a more streamlined appearance.

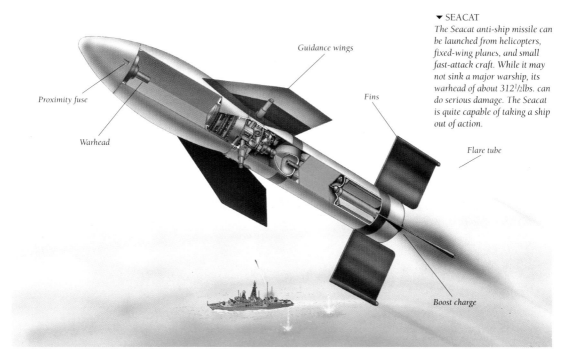

The Seacat anti-ship missile can be launched from helicopters, fixed-wing planes, and small fast-attack craft. While it may not sink a major warship, its warhead of about 312$\frac{1}{2}$lbs. can do serious damage. The Seacat is quite capable of taking a ship out of action.

Guidance wings

Proximity fuse

Fins

Warhead

Flare tube

Boost charge

ballistic missiles (SSBNs). The United States Navy has the largest number of SSBNs in the world.

In March 1992 the U.S. Navy decommissioned the last operational battleship in the world, the U.S.S. *Missouri*. The 45,000-ton *Missouri* was launched in 1944 and served in the Pacific during World War II and later in the Korean War. The *Missouri* was armed with nine 16inch guns. These were last used in action as recently as 1991, when the battleship bombarded Iraqi positions in Kuwait during the Gulf War.

▼ BROADSIDE
A *Missouri*-class battleship lets rip a broadside with her 16inch guns. The guns have a maximum range of 136,450 feet and fire an 2125lb. shell. The U.S. Navy was the last force to use battleships in action.

Key Dates

- 1914–1918 World War I.

- 1914, November 1: Battle of the Coronel.

- 1914, December 8: Battle of the Falklands.

- 1916, May 31: Battle of Jutland.

- 1939, December 13: Battle of the River Plate.

- 1941, May 27: Sinking of the *Bismarck*.

- 1944, June 6: D-Day.

- 1945, April 7: Sinking of the battleship *Yamato*.

Smaller Fighting Ships

▲ PATROL
A warship fires one of its Harpoon missiles.

THERE WAS SHOCK and surprise among senior naval officers in both North America and Europe when the first torpedo boat was launched in 1878. It was the 19-knot British-built *Lightning,* with a torpedo tube in its bow. This compact torpedo boat had the speed and fire power to race after larger ships and to sink or damage them.

Japanese torpedo boats proved very effective against the Russians in the Russo-Japanese War during nighttime action at Wei-Hai-Wei in 1895 and again at Port Arthur on February 8, 1904.

In World War I the British Royal Navy deployed coastal motor boats (CMBs) and motor launches (MLs) in the narrows of the English Channel.

▶ PATROL
U.S. warships patrol, their masts cluttered with radar and radio antennae.

During World War II the German motor torpedo boats were designated *S-Boot,* or *Schnellboot,* meaning "fast boat." They were known by their crews as *Eilboot (E-Boot)* meaning "boat in a hurry." Several classes of *S-Boot* were built. Most were powered by three-shaft Daimler–Benz or MAN diesel engines and had a maximum speed of 39–42 knots with a range of 220 miles.

World War II armament was varied, but for most of the war it consisted of two .8inch antiaircraft (AA) guns and two 21inch torpedo tubes. From 1944, defensive armament was upgraded and became one $1\frac{1}{2}$inch and three .8inch AA guns, or one $1\frac{1}{2}$inch and five .8inch AA guns.

Larger types of ship could also carry six or eight mines in place of reloading torpedoes.

During World War II, John F. Kennedy, the future President of the United States, commanded a U.S. Navy patrol torpedo

INDIVIDUAL SHIPS

The anti-ship missile and torpedo have given smaller craft a powerful punch, making them a dangerous enemy for larger, slow-moving naval vessels. Modern materials and improved engine design give these craft a performance similar to racing speedboats. They are able to dart toward larger, slower ships, launch their missiles, and retreat very quickly.

▼ SAETTIA
An Italian Saettia-class small-missile craft has a crew of 33 and a maximum speed of 40 knots and weighs 400 tons fully loaded.

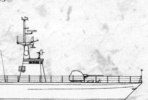

▼ PATRA
A French Patra-class craft has a crew of 18 and a maximum speed of 26 knots and weighs 147.5 tons fully loaded.

▼ SPICA
A Swedish Spica II-class torpedo attack craft has a crew of 27 and a maximum speed of 40.5 knots and weighs 230 tons fully loaded.

◀ PATROL BOAT
Small nations with coastlines to protect make extensive use of patrol craft such as this one. These boats are used to police maritime borders and for anti-piracy and anti-smuggling operations.

(PT) boat in the Pacific. The boat was powered by three gasoline engines which gave it a maximum speed of 40 knots.

The surface-to-surface missile was developed after World War II and gave small craft new hitting power. The postwar Soviet Osa ships were capable of speeds up to 38 knots and were armed with four SS-N-2A "Styx" missiles. Nearly 300 Osas were built and were used to equip 20 navies throughout the world. Osas saw action in the Middle East in the 1973 Yom Kippur War between Israel and her Arab neighbors, and also in the Gulf War in 1990–1991.

Patrol boats are ideal for landing small groups of special forces. These kinds of attack are usually undercover, amphibious attacks. Patrol boats are also widely used in peacetime for search and rescue missions, fishery patrols, and anti-piracy operations.

◀ KNOX
A U.S. Knox-class frigate has a crew of 300, and a maximum speed of 27 knots and weighs 4,260 tons fully loaded. It is armed with guns, torpedoes, and missiles. Knox-class frigates are no longer in service with the U.S. navy, but are still used by smaller nations.

▼ TESTS
Verifier, a British Aerospace trials craft, launches a Sea Skua anti-ship missile during evaluation trials. Missiles such as the 362lb. Sea Skua with its 22½lb. warhead, although originally designed as an airborne anti-ship missile, give even the smallest craft a considerable punch.

Key Dates

- 1878 *Lightning* 19-knot torpedo boat launched.
- 1914–1918 World War I: British Royal Navy coastal motor boats and launches reach 35 knots.
- 1939–1945 World War II: German E-boats reach 42 knots.
- 1958 Soviet Komar class missile-armed craft enter service.
- 1966 Soviet Osa-class missile-armed craft enter service.
- 1973 Soviet Osa-class craft see action in the Middle East.
- 1990–1991 Osa class craft see action in the Gulf War.

Submarines

▲ THE *TURTLE*
This hand-propelled craft was devised by the American David Bushnell in the early 19th century.

THE FIRST SUBMARINE attack was carried out during the Civil War by a semi-submersible steam-propelled Confederate craft called *David*. It damaged a Federal ironclad ship with a spar torpedo. No one would have guessed that this crude underwater craft would be the forerunner of the most sophisticated and powerful weapons that the world has ever known.

Electric and oil fuel motors made fully submersible boats practical. In 1886 Lt. Isaac Peral of Spain built an electrically powered boat. The following year the Russians built a boat armed with four torpedoes. In 1895 the streamlined *Plunger* was built in the United States by John Holland. On the surface it used a steam engine to charge the batteries that powered it when moving underwater.

The German U-boats in World War I showed how submarine warfare could be a strategic weapon in attacking commercial shipping as well as launching tactical attacks on enemy warships.

On August 8, 1914, the U-15 fired a torpedo at the battleship H.M.S. *Monarch*. Although the torpedo missed, it was the first time that an automotive torpedo had been fired against an enemy from a submarine.

In World War II the Germans capitalized on this experience by concentrating U-boats into "wolf packs" to attack British convoys in the North Atlantic. The Allies were able to defeat the U-boats by breaking the coded signals transmitted to them and by using improved detection systems and weapons. In the Pacific, the U.S. Navy waged a highly effective submarine campaign against Japanese commercial and naval ships.

In the postwar years nuclear power changed submarines forever. Now they could, in theory, stay submerged for indefinite periods of time. The first

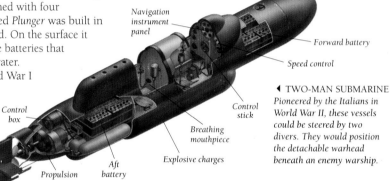

Navigation instrument panel
Forward battery
Speed control
Control box
Control stick
Breathing mouthpiece
Explosive charges
Aft battery
Propulsion motor

◀ TWO-MAN SUBMARINE
Pioneered by the Italians in World War II, these vessels could be steered by two divers. They would position the detachable warhead beneath an enemy warship.

HUNTER KILLER

Modern submarines are divided into two classes: the nuclear-powered submarines armed with nuclear missiles (SSBNs) and the hunter killers (SSNs). The latter may attack enemy surface ships, but they are also very effective at hunting SSBNs. In World War II Allied submarines made torpedo attacks on surfaced enemy U-boats. However, modern SSNs can hunt and kill underwater, using sonar to locate the enemy and firing sophisticated guided torpedoes.

▼ DIESEL POWER
A diesel-powered hunter-killer submarine. Diesel power is a very quiet form of propulsion.

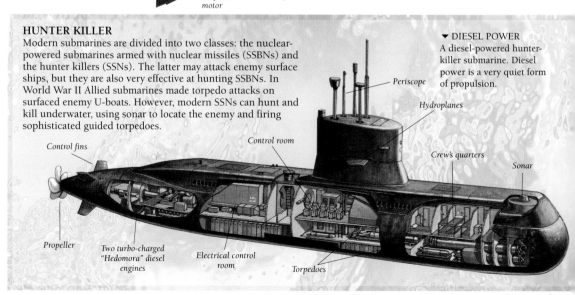

Periscope
Hydroplanes
Control room
Crew's quarters
Sonar
Control fins
Propeller
Two turbo-charged "Hedomora" diesel engines
Electrical control room
Torpedoes

nuclear submarine was the U.S.S. *Nautilus*. It was commissioned in 1954 and could dive to more than 650 feet. In 1959 the launch of the U.S.S. *George Washington* marked the arrival of the world's most formidable weapon. This nuclear-powered submarine was armed with Polaris nuclear missiles which could be launched while the boat was submerged.

On May 2, 1982, off the Falklands, the submarine H.M.S. *Conquerer* torpedoed and sank the Argentinian heavy cruiser *General Belgrano*. Despite the use of very efficient anti-submarine tracking systems and weapons, submarines remain a powerful weapon because of the secret nature of their operations.

▶ BOMBER
An SSBN is known in the British Royal Navy as a "bomber." Its missiles are housed in launch tubes astern of the fin, or conning tower.

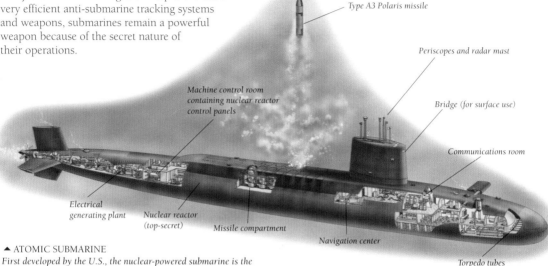

Type A3 Polaris missile

Periscopes and radar mast

Machine control room containing nuclear reactor control panels

Bridge (for surface use)

Communications room

Electrical generating plant

Nuclear reactor (top-secret)

Missile compartment

Navigation center

Torpedo tubes

▲ ATOMIC SUBMARINE
First developed by the U.S., the nuclear-powered submarine is the most powerful warship in history. It is armed with intercontinental nuclear missiles which can be fired from underwater.

▼ NEGATIVE BUOYANCY
A submarine dives by letting water into its buoyancy tanks, and this makes it heavy enough to sink. To surface it "blows" its tanks, pushing air into them so that the water is forced out.

Buoyancy tanks full

Buoyancy tanks flood, and submarine sinks

Buoyancy tanks filled with air, expelling the water, and the submarine surfaces

Key Dates

- 1863 October 5: steam-driven submersible *David* attacks Federal ironclad ship.

- 1895 U.S.S. *Plunger*, the first battery-powered boat.

- 1904 *Aigret*, first diesel-powered boat.

- 1914–1918 World War I German U-boats wage war against Allied commercial shipping.

- 1939–1945 World War II German U-boats use "wolf pack" tactics against Allied shipping.

- 1954 U.S.S. *Nautilus*, the first nuclear-powered submarine, is commissioned.

Aircraft Carriers

▲ VERTICAL
A Royal Navy Harrier takes off in the Falklands in 1982.

ARLY AIRPLANES WERE FRAGILE and underpowered. They were still a dangerous and risky form of transportation when U.S. airman Eugene Ely made the first successful flight from a platform rigged on the deck of a U.S. Navy cruiser in 1911. Two months later the intrepid Ely also made a landing on board a ship. He had effectively become the first carrier pilot, although at that time aircraft carriers did not yet exist.

In 1913 H.M.S. *Hermes* pioneered aircraft carrier design with its short flying-off deck and three airplanes. A U-boat sank her in 1914, but her successor, completed in 1919, was a true aircraft carrier. During World War I the British used seaplane carriers from which aircraft were lowered into the sea.

The interwar years saw a rapid development in carrier design and capability. H.M.S. *Ark Royal*, which was commissioned in 1938, incorporated all the latest features: arrester wire to halt incoming aircraft, net crash barrier, batsmen to guide pilots, and catapults to launch aircraft. In 1939 Britain had ten carriers. In 1941 Japan had eleven, and the U.S. had three. By the end of the war the U.S. Navy had over 100 in action.

At Taranto, Italy, in 1940, 21 Swordfish aircraft from the British Royal Navy carrier H.M.S. *Illustrious* attacked ships of the Italian Navy, severely damaging three battleships. The Japanese are believed to have modeled their attack at Pearl Harbor on December 7, 1941, on Taranto. They committed 360 aircraft armed with torpedoes and bombs, and sank or immobilized eight battleships, three cruisers, and other craft. The U.S. Navy carrier fleet, which was at sea at the time of the attack, formed the nucleus of a new Pacific fleet.

In May 1942, the U.S. Navy fought the Battle of the Coral Sea against the Japanese. It was the first sea battle fought entirely by aircraft attacking ships. In June 1942,

▲ TAKE-OFF
A British RNAS Sopwith Pup fighter planes takes off during trials in World War I.

LARGE AND SMALL
In the 20th century aircraft carriers have grown from simple "flat tops" to virtual cities at sea. The U.S.S. *Nimitz*, for example, has a crew of more than 6,000 with 50 planes as well as helicopters. In World War I H.M.S. *Hermes* was the first planes carrier and had only three planes. *Hermes* was sunk by a U-boat; even today aircraft carriers are vulnerable to submarine attack.

◀ LAUNCHING
This McDonnell Douglas Hornet is preparing to take off.

◀ SIZE
A huge U.S. carrier is maneuvered into harbour by small tugboats.

▲ ARRESTING
A McDonnell Douglas Hornet hits an arrester net.

▲ FIGHTER POWER
McDonnell Hornet fighters aboard a US carrier. The Hornet's six Phalanx missiles can be used against six targets simultaneously.

the Battle of Midway was another complex air and sea action. These two battles cost the Japanese six of their ten carriers, and the U.S. Navy four of the original eight.

After 1945, more enhancements were incorporated into carrier design. The addition of helicopters allowed carriers to launch operations against enemy submarines and also to land marines to secure coastal positions. The angled flight deck allowed aircraft to take off while others were landing. In 1961 the U.S.S. *Enterprise* was completed—at 75,700 tons it was the largest aircraft carrier ever built. It could carry 100 aircraft and, being nuclear-powered, had a cruising range the equivalent of 20 times around the world.

In 1967 the British decided that they would phase out fixed-wing aircraft in favor of the Vertical Short Take-Off and Landing (VSTOL) BAe Sea Harrier. The upward-angled ski-slope deck made takeoffs easier for Harriers, and subsequently both Italy and Spain have adopted this less expensive option of a carrier equipped with Harriers. In the mid-1970s the Soviet Union began building carriers equipped with VSTOL Yakovlev Yak-36MP "Forger" aircraft and helicopters.

Carriers were involved in the Korean War, at Suez in 1956, in Vietnam, in the Falklands, and in the Gulf War of 1990–1991.

▼ CARRIER POWER
This U.S. Navy Kitty Hawk-class conventionally powered carrier has a crew of nearly 6,000. It can carry up to 50 planes, including F-14 Tomcats and F-18 Hornets, as well as helicopters.

▼ BATTLE GROUP
A modern naval battle group is built up around a carrier, with supporting vessels to provide cover against enemy aircraft, surface vessels, and submarines. The carrier's combat aircraft can attack ships and installations at a safe range from the group.

Key Dates

- 1911 Eugene Ely flies off a ship.
- 1913 H.M.S. *Hermes* is commissioned.
- 1940 November 11: British Fleet Air Arm air attack on Italian fleet at Taranto.
- 1941 December 7: Japanese carrier aircraft attack U.S. Navy in Pearl Harbor.
- 1942 May: Major carrier action in Battle of the Coral Sea.
- 1942 June 4–7: Battle of Midway.
- 1961 U.S.S. *Enterprise* is first nuclear-powered carrier.

Early Fighter Planes

THE EARLY PILOTS were often wealthy and enterprising sportsmen, so the idea of shooting at each other in war was considered to be ungentlemanly. However, it was not long before pilots carried rifles and pistols when flying, and took pot shots at each other. The first true fighter action took place during World War I on October 5, 1914, when a French Voisin V89 brought down a German Aviatik aircraft with its machine-gun fire.

The interrupter gear invented by the Dutchman Anthony Fokker allowed German aircraft to fire forward through the arc of their propeller. This meant that fighter pilots could aim their aircraft at enemy planes.

▶ FOKKER TRIPLANE
The German World War I Fokker Dr-I fighter had a maximum speed of 24mph and was armed with two .31 inch Spandau machine guns.

Between 1914 and 1918 aircraft speeds increased from 105mph to 168mph. The first fighters flew at a height of 13,000 feet, but by the end of the war they were up to 19,700 feet.

One of the most successful British fighters was the SE-5a. It had a maximum speed of 41mph and was armed with a single synchronized Vickers or Lewis machine gun. The German D1 Albatross had a maximum speed of 34mph and was armed with twin .31inch Spandau machine guns.

The interwar period saw the development of the all-metal aircraft with wing-mounted machine guns and also cannon that fired explosive rounds. By 1939 the Messerschmitt Bf-109E had a top speed of 355mph, and by 1945 the 109G with a 1,900hp inline engine had a top speed of 428mph. Armament was a 1¼ inch cannon and two .31 inch machine guns.

The World War II Allied fighters, the British Supermarine Spitfire, and the North American P-51 Mustang were classic types. The Mustang, fitted with

FIGHTERS OF THE WORLD WARS

Early fighters were slow scout planes with simple armament. By the beginning of World War II they were all-metal monoplanes with cannon as well as machine guns. By the close of the war the first jet fighters were in action, and many aircraft were equipped with radar.

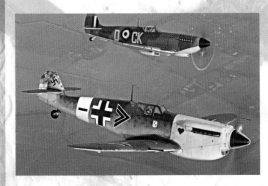

◀ BATTLE OF BRITAIN
A Spitfire with a postwar Merlin-engined Messerschmitt Me-109 photographed during the film *The Battle of Britain*. Spain used the Messerschmitt 109 after the war but put in new engines to improve its performance.

▲ P-38 LIGHTNING
With a top speed of 414mph the Lockheed Lightning, introduced in 1941, was armed with four machine guns and a .8 inch cannon. It could carry 4500lbs. of bombs.

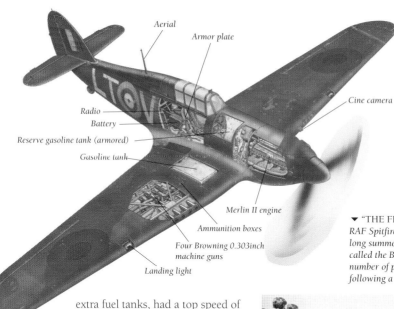

Aerial

Armor plate

Radio

Battery

Reserve gasoline tank (armored)

Gasoline tank

Cine camera

Merlin II engine

Ammunition boxes

Four Browning 0.303inch
machine guns

Landing light

◀ HAWKER HURRICANE
*Armed with eight .303inch
machine guns, the Hurricane
was older and slower than the
Spitfire. However, it shot down
more German planes during
the Battle of Britain than the
Spitfire did. Hurricane pilots
concentrated on attacking the
slower, more vulnerable
bombers, while Spitfires fought
with the escorting
Messerschmitt 109 fighters.*

▼ "THE FEW"
*RAF Spitfire pilots wait on an airstrip in the
long summer air battle of 1940 that was
called the Battle of Britain. The small
number of pilots were nicknamed "The Few"
following a speech by Winston Churchill.*

extra fuel tanks, had a top speed of
437mph and sufficient range to allow
pilots to escort bombers to Berlin and back. The Spitfire
went through 21 different marks between 1936 and
1945, becoming a more powerful and more heavily
armed fighter with each version. The Spitfire MIX,
powered by a Rolls-Royce 1,660hp Merlin engine, had
a top speed of 657kph and was armed with .303inch
machine guns and .8 inch cannon.

Some of the fighters continued in service into the
1950s and 1960s as ground-attack aircraft. Those
fighter aircraft that are still flying today are in the hands
of aviation enthusiasts.

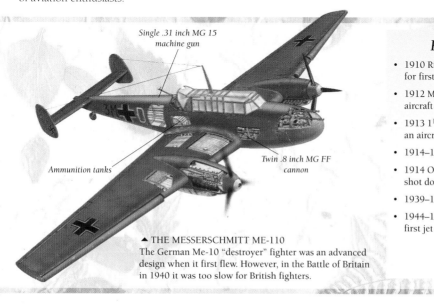

Single .31 inch MG 15
machine gun

Ammunition tanks

Twin .8 inch MG FF
cannon

▲ THE MESSERSCHMITT ME-110
The German Me-10 "destroyer" fighter was an advanced
design when it first flew. However, in the Battle of Britain
in 1940 it was too slow for British fighters.

Key Dates

- 1910 Rifle fired from an aircraft
  for first time.
- 1912 Machine gun fired from
  aircraft for first time.
- 1913 $1\frac{1}{2}$ inch cannon fired from
  an aircraft.
- 1914–1918 World War I.
- 1914 October 5: first plane to be
  shot down.
- 1939–1945 World War II.
- 1944–1945 Me-262, the world's
  first jet fighter.

Jet Fighters

▲ FLYING HIGH
An F-15 Eagle pilot in the cockpit

DURING THE 1930S aircraft powered by jet propulsion featured in science fiction comics, along with men from Mars and moon rockets. However, both the British and the Germans were conducting research in this field before World War II. The first jet to fly was the German He-178 in 1939, followed by the British Gloster Meteor, which flew fitted with jet engines in 1941. The two planes never met in combat, but science fiction became reality in 1944 when RAF Meteors took to the air to chase and shoot down German V-1 flying bombs.

Deliveries of the world's first operational jet-powered fighter, the German Messerschmitt Me-262 *Schwalbe* (Swallow), began in May 1944. However, these aircraft were initially configured as bombers, and the fighter did not enter service until later that year. It had a maximum speed of 540mph and was armed with four 1¼inch cannons, and 24 2inch R4M rockets. Me-262s took a heavy toll of U.S. Army Air Force (USAAF) bombers during 1945. On the Allied side, the Gloster Meteor had a maximum speed of 410mph and was armed with four 8inch cannons.

The Korean War saw the first jet-versus-jet action when U.S. Air Force F-86 Sabres, F-80 Shooting Stars and U.S. Marine Corps F9F Panthers fought with Chinese MiG-15s. The first victory went to a U.S. Air Force (USAF) F-80 Shooting Star on November 8, 1950 against a Chinese MiG-15 over the Yalu River.

Jet fighters have been in action, either in air combat or attacking ground targets, in most parts of the world since the 1950s. Over North Vietnam, in the conflicts between India and Pakistan, in the Arab–Israeli wars, in the Gulf Wars between Iran and Iraq, and between the Coalition Forces and Iraq, U.S.-designed aircraft have fought with Soviet aircraft. In the Falklands in 1982 British Harriers were pitted against U.S. and French-designed aircraft. Soviet jet aircraft were used in ground attack operations during the Afghan War.

Among the most versatile jet fighter aircraft are the Russian MiG-21 and the American McDonnell Douglas F-4 Phantom, which

◀ FIGHTING FALCON
The American F-16 Fighting Falcon multi-role fighter is made by General Dynamics, and is in service in more than 14 countries worldwide. Painted in striking livery, it is flown by the USAF Thunderbirds display team.

A NEW BREED OF WAR PLANE
Immediately after World War II there was a move to design and build jet fighters. U.S. and Chinese jets clashed in the Korean War in 1950–1953. Although missiles such as the Sidewinder have been widely used in combat, the 1¼ inch cannon is still a very effective weapon and can be used against ground targets.

◀ MIRAGE 5
The French Dassault fighter has a top speed of 1,188mph. Operating in a ground-attack role, the Mirage can carry bombs, rockets, or missiles.

▼ PHANTOM
The F-4 Phantom has been built in larger numbers than any Western combat aircraft since World War II.

▲ F86 SABRE
The first woman to fly faster than sound, Jacqueline Cochran, achieved the record in a Sabre on May 18, 1953.

▲ HAWK
The British BAe Hawk is a versatile combat plane which can also be used as a trainer.

Weapons system
ranging radar

IFF aerials
(identification
friend or foe)

Koliesov lift
engines

GSh-23L
cannon pack

▼ FORGER
*The Russian Yak-38, or "Forger," was a vertical
take-off combat plane that first flew in 1971.*

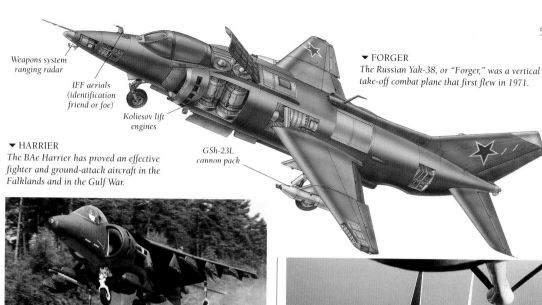

▼ HARRIER
*The BAe Harrier has proved an effective
fighter and ground-attack aircraft in the
Falklands and in the Gulf War.*

have fought in Vietnam and the Middle East.

In many of these combats the AIM-9 Sidewinder
heat-seeking air-to-air missile has been the key
weapon. The AIM-9 heat-seeking missile takes its
inspiration from nature. The sidewinder snake locates
its prey by detecting their body heat with special
sensors in its head. The AIM-9 Sidewinder missile
detects the heat from the engine exhausts of its target.

▲ EAGLE
*A missile-armed USAF McDonnell Douglas F-15 Eagle multi-role
fighter maneuvers into position during in-flight refueling.*

▼ EUROFIGHTER
Built by a consortium of Spain, Germany, Italy, and Britain, the Eurofighter Typhoon
first flew on March 29, 1994. The project has been hampered by political problems
because Germany has reduced its requirement and has argued for a less expensive
aircraft now that the Cold War has ended.

Key Dates

- 1939 German Heinkel He-178 jet fighter flies

- 1944 German Me-262 enters service

- 1944 British Gloster Meteor in action against V-1 flying bombs

- 1944 Lockheed Shooting Star enters service with USAAF/USAF

- 1945 December 3: De Havilland Vampire makes first jet landing and takeoff from a carrier

- 1950 First jet-versus-jet victory in Korean War

- 1966 August 31: Hawker Harrier makes first hovering flight

Early Bombers

THE POTENTIAL FOR AIRCRAFT to operate as a platform for delivering bombs to enemy targets was realized as early as 1911. In that year the first bombs were dropped from an aircraft during the Italo-Turkish war.

In World War I bombers started as scout planes, in which the crew had taken a few grenades to lob at the enemy lines. Bombers grew from these small single-engined two-seater aircraft to types such as the British Handley Page 0/400. Around 550 of these twin-engined bombers were built. When they attacked German military and industrial targets, they flew in formations of 30–40 aircraft.

The German Gotha GIV and GV bombers attacked targets in London and southern England in World War I. They carried between 750lbs. and 1250lbs. of bombs, had a crew of three, and were capable of 109mph with a range of 373 miles.

In the interwar period there was considerable fear that bombers carrying bombs loaded with poison gas would attack large cities, causing huge casualties. The German Air Force was re-formed secretly after World War I, and the sleek Heinkel He-111 and Dornier Do 17, both described as airliners, were re-engineered as bombers for World War II. The He-111 carried 6250lbs. of bombs and the Do 17 2500lbs. The Junkers Ju 87 became notorious as the Stuka dive bomber, and the Ju 88 made the transition from bomber to heavily armed fighter.

▲ LANCASTER
The British bomber was used in the "Dam Buster" raids against Germany.

◀ HANDLEY PAGE 0/400
With a crew of three the RAF Handley Page 0/400 could carry up to 2,250lbs. of bombs. It was armed with up to five .303inch Lewis machine guns.

BOMBERS OF THE WORLD WARS

In the two World Wars the payload and range of bombers increased dramatically. At the beginning of World War II the German He-111 was carrying 6250lbs. of bombs at 261mph. By the close of World War II the four-engined Avro Lancaster was carrying 15,875lbs. of bombs at 287mph for 1,600 miles.

◀ B-25 MITCHELL
A U.S. Mitchell medium bomber escorted by a Vought F-4U Corsair carrier-based fighter. The Mitchell could carry 3500lbs. of bombs. Several examples of Mitchells have been restored in the U.S.

▲ LANCASTER
The RAF Avro Lancaster entered service in March 1942 and became the mainstay of the bombing campaign against Germany. By 1944 there were 40 Lancaster squadrons in action.

▶ B-17 FLYING FORTRESS
The B-17 could carry 6,750lbs. of bombs
at 312mph. By the end of the war over
4,700 were in front line service with the USAAF.

On the Allied side, bombers grew in size, range, and bomb load. In 1939, the Vickers Wellington could carry 7500lbs. of bombs. By 1945 the Avro Lancaster could carry 15,875lbs. of bombs to 1,658 miles. The USAAF Boeing B-17 had a maximum bomb load of 14,500lbs. and a range of 3,298 miles. The Consolidated B-24 Liberator carried up to 9,000lbs. of bombs at 300mph.

Supporters of strategic bombing say that it made a major contribution to the Allied victory in World War II. However, despite the importance of bombing, history has shown that victory is guaranteed only when ground forces enter enemy territory and occupy it.

▼ DRESDEN 1945
German authorities sort through bodies in the ghastly aftermath of the attack on Dresden. Attacked by 773 RAF bombers by night and by the USAAF during the day, nearly 8 square miles were destroyed by fire. In the overcrowded city more than 100,000 died in the firestorm.

Key Dates

- 1911 Bombs first dropped in the Italo-Turkish War.

- 1914–1918 World War I: tactical and rudimentary strategic bombing established.

- 1936–1939 Spanish Civil War: tactical bombing perfected.

- 1939–1945 World War II: first strategic bombing.

- 1942 Pressurized B-29 Superfortress flies.

- 1944–1945 German Arado 234 jet bomber in action.

- 1945 Atomic bombs dropped on Japan by B-29s.

Modern Jets and Stealth

THE CLOAK OF INVISIBILITY is a feature of many ancient myths. Although it may not be a reality, new techniques in aircraft design have made planes very hard to detect by systems such as radar. These features are known as "stealth," and all modern combat aircraft now have some stealth features. Stealth in aircraft design is the attempt to minimize the ways in which aircraft can be detected by ground or airborne air defense systems.

In its earliest form, camouflage paint was a stealth feature, but the echo from radar would show the location of the most ingeniously camouflaged plane. One technique for defeating early radars was to fly very low and so hide the aircraft among the clutter of radar echoes. Modern radars can now discriminate between clutter and moving targets, so the next move was to design a plane that gave very little or no radar return. This was achieved by giving the plane as few surfaces as possible

from which a radar beam could bounce off and so give an echo. Besides having a profile designed to avoid radar, the plane was coated with a radar-absorbent material which would further reduce or limit the echo. If there is no discernible radar echo, the heat from

▲ NIGHTHAWK
The Lockheed F-117A Nighthawk first saw action in 1989 in Panama and later in 1991 in the Gulf. An F-117 was shot down over the former Yugoslavia in 1999.

▶ STEALTH
The Lockheed/Boeing F-22A Rapier, the new fighter for the USAF, has "stealth" features within its design.

MODERN DEVELOPMENTS
Radar and thermal detection systems have made combat aircraft vulnerable, even if they are flying low and at night. Since radar reflects off flat hard surfaces, any plane with a less angular shape and a "radar-absorbent" coating is less likely to be detected. The engines produce hot gases which can be picked up by radar. However, these gases can be cooled or screened before they pass into the air.

F-107 WR-400 turbofan jet engine

Folding wings

Nuclear warhead

Tercom guidance system

▶ SCALE MODEL
A wind-tunnel model of an American experimental combat aircraft. Computer modeling is used to evaluate new designs.

▲ CRUISE MISSILE
The German V-1, the earliest cruise missile, was slow and fairly inaccurate. In the late 1970s the United States produced a cruise missile that could be launched from land, sea, or air. It has a guidance system that is very accurate and can fly a circuitous route to its target. Cruise missiles have been used in the Middle East and Serbia.

▼ FIGHTER
The Boeing Joint Strike Fighter will replace several types of combat aircraft from 2004.

▶ BOEING B-52
The veteran USAF B-52 strategic bomber has been used since 1955. It can carry up to 22,680kg of air - launched cruise missiles or 51 1,135lb. conventional bombs.

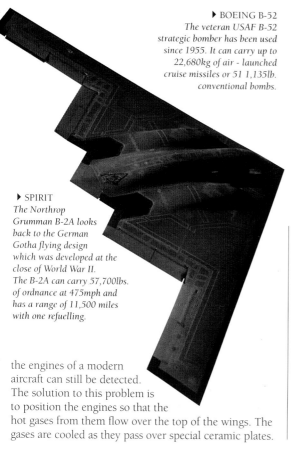

▶ SPIRIT
The Northrop Grumman B-2A looks back to the German Gotha flying design which was developed at the close of World War II. The B-2A can carry 57,700lbs. of ordnance at 475mph and has a range of 11,500 miles with one refuelling.

the engines of a modern aircraft can still be detected. The solution to this problem is to position the engines so that the hot gases from them flow over the top of the wings. The gases are cooled as they pass over special ceramic plates.

The classic stealth aircraft are the U.S. Lockheed F-117 fighter, which was used in action in 1989 as a bomber in the invasion of Panama and later in attacks on Iraq in 1991. An F-117 was shot down during the air attacks on Serbia in 1999.

The Northrop B-2 Advanced Technology Bomber is a dedicated stealth bomber. It is capable of carrying 42,300lbs. of ordnance over a maximum range of 6,096 miles.

The USAF Advanced Tactical Fighter program took place in the 1990s. It was a competition between the Lockheed/General Dynamics YF-22 and the McDonnell Douglas YF-23, two fighters with stealth features. The Lockheed aircraft, now designated the F-22 Rapier, has been accepted and will enter service by 2011.

▼ STEALTH TECHNOLOGY
Although stealth is associated with aircraft, it has also been employed in the design of modern combat ships and even in tanks. Ships and tanks can be detected on radar and thermal imaging, so their exhausts need to be screened and any radar-reflective surfaces have to be softened.

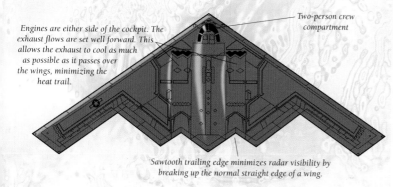

Engines are either side of the cockpit. The exhaust flows are set well forward. This allows the exhaust to cool as much as possible as it passes over the wings, minimizing the heat trail.

Two-person crew compartment

Sawtooth trailing edge minimizes radar visibility by breaking up the normal straight edge of a wing.

Key Dates

- 1951 Canberra bomber is the first jet to fly across the North Atlantic nonstop.
- 1955 B-52 enters service with the USAF.
- 1977 December: first flight of Lockheed Martin F-117.
- 1983–1984 U.S. stealth research ship *Sea Shadow* built.
- 1989 July 17: first flight of Northrop Grumman B-2A Spirit.
- 1991 March 14: Smyge Swedish stealth patrol craft launched.
- 1991 April: F-22 Rapier selected by USAF.

Airborne Troops

▲ PARACHUTE
The light fabric of a parachute traps air, slowing down the descent of the soldier or paratrooper.

I T IS HARD FOR US to realize how unusual paratroops seemed when they first appeared, in World War II. Most soldiers had never traveled in an airplane, so men who arrived by parachute from planes seemed almost as fantastic as spacemen. The Soviet Union pioneered airborne forces in the interwar years. However, it was Nazi Germany that made first use of them in World War II.

Airborne troops could be delivered to the battlefield either by parachute or in gliders. Troop-carrying gliders carried between 10 and 29 troops and could also be used to transport vehicles and light artillery. They were particularly effective when an operation called for a formed group of men to attack a target such as a bridge or coastal artillery battery. The problem with paratroops was that they could be scattered over a large area if they jumped from too high a position.

The German attack on the island of Crete in May 1941 involved 22,500 paratroops and 80 gliders. The airborne forces suffered very heavy losses: 4,000 were killed, 2,000 wounded, and 220 aircraft were destroyed. Hitler declared that "the day of the

paratrooper is over." The Americans and British were quick to learn from the Germans' mistakes, and airborne forces were used on D-Day in Normandy in June 1944. Airborne forces were also in Sicily in 1943, and at the Rhine crossings in 1945. In Burma in 1943, British and Commonwealth troops known as Chindits were landed by glider deep inside Japanese lines. In this way they drew Japanese forces away from the front lines in India.

After World War II, the French made extensive use of paratroops in Indochina (Vietnam) between 1948 and 1954. However, in May 1954 at

▶ PARATROOPER
A British paratrooper in World War II. The buckle in the middle of his chest operates as a quick release for the parachute harness.

AIRBORNE OPERATIONS
Attacks by paratroops and glider-borne soldiers in World War II were sometimes a gamble, because these lightly equipped soldiers could be defeated by ground troops with tanks and artillery. If friendly ground forces could link up with them, airborne troops could sieze and hold key positions such as bridges, fortifications, and causeways. They could help to keep up the momentum of an attack.

▲ JUMPING FOR FUN
A sports parachutist exits from an aircraft in the "spread stable position." Before he pulls the release on his parachute he will enjoy a period of "free fall."

▶ TRANSPORTATION
Transport planes can carry trucks and vehicles which can be unloaded if a suitable airfield has been captured and secured.

▲ DROP ZONE
Parachutes float down and collapse in a mass military drop. The flat area allocated for such an operation is called a drop zone, or DZ. Helicopters put down soldiers on a landing zone, or LZ.

Dien Bien Phu they were defeated when they set up an airborne base deep inside Viet Minh lines. They lost 11 complete parachute battalions in the fighting.

On November 5, 1956 French and British paratroops landed at Port Said to recapture the Suez Canal, which had been nationalized by the Egyptians.

Today, helicopters mean troops no longer need to parachute from aircraft. However, airborne forces are still considered an elite group within all national armies.

▲ SEALS
These Seals, U.S. Navy Special Forces troops, are wearing harnesses that clip onto a ladder. They are being lifted by a Chinook helicopter.

▶ HOW A PARACHUTE WORKS
The umbrella shape of the parachute, called a canopy, was first made from silk; later, nylon. It traps air and so slows the descent of the parachutist or cargo. A small hole in the center canopy allows air to escape and prevents the parachute from swinging from side to side.

Modern square parachutes are called "ram air." They can be steered, allowing the parachutist to land with very great accuracy. The latest development is a remotely controlled steerable canopy which can be used by special forces in remote locations to take delivery of cargo. The load is dropped at a great height.

Key Dates

- 1797 Parachute invented.
- 1927 Italians are first to drop a "stick" of paratroops.
- 1930s Soviet forces develop paratroops.
- 1939–1945 Airborne operations in Europe and Far East.
- 1941 German airborne attack on island of Crete.
- 1944 British and Polish landings at Arnhem.
- 1953–1954 Battle of Dien Bien Phu in Vietnam.
- 1956 French and British paratroops capture Suez Canal.

Helicopters

▲ SEA KNIGHT
A U.S. Marine Corps Sea Knight with an underslung load lifts off.

A S THEY CLATTER IN AND OUT of heliports, helicopters are an everyday sight. Most people think that they are a postwar invention. However, the first free flight by a tandem-rotor device was by Paul Cornu on November 13, 1907. Igor Sikorsky built two helicopters in Russia in 1909–1910.

Helicopters were used at the close of World War II, and in Korea and Indo-China the Americans and French used them to evacuate wounded soldiers from the battlefield. The most widely used helicopters in this period were the Sikorsky H-19 and the Bell H-13 Sioux. On November 5, 1956, at the Suez Canal, British Royal Marines were landed by helicopter in the first airborne assault. In the Algerian war of 1954–1962 the French used helicopters to carry troops. The helicopters were fitted with anti-tank missiles and machine guns.

The American involvement in Vietnam, from 1962 to 1975, saw the use of helicopters in assault, casualty evacuation, and transportation and liaison missions. In airborne assaults 16 troop-carrying helicopters nicknamed "Slicks" were supported by 9 attack

▲ APACHE
The U.S. Army's Apache attack helicopter has a crew of two and a maximum speed of 227mph.

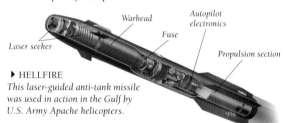

Laser seeker, Warhead, Fuse, Autopilot electronics, Propulsion section

▶ HELLFIRE
This laser-guided anti-tank missile was used in action in the Gulf by U.S. Army Apache helicopters.

VERTICAL FLIGHT
Helicopters are used in wartime to transport troops, casualties, and supplies. They can rescue shot-down pilots and attack ships, submarines, and ground targets. Some are even equipped for air-to-air combat.

▲ TRANSPORT
The Boeing Vertol CH-47 Chinook has a crew of two and can carry up to 44 troops.

▲ RESCUE
A British Royal Navy GKN Westland Sea King has airborne early-warning radar to warn surface ships about enemy missiles or warships. The Sea King can also winch people from the sea.

▼ OSPREY
The American Bell Boeing Osprey tilt-rotor aircraft can carry up to 24 combat-equipped troops or 22,675lbs. of cargo. The U.S. Marine Corps was an enthusiastic advocate of the Osprey, which can transport troops quickly from offshore to secure beachheads.

▶ BLACKHAWK
The Sikorsky UH-60 Blackhawk has a crew of two and can carry 12 soldiers.

Hellfire missiles

Rotor head

Rotor mast

Blade pitch control rods

Electronics bay

Solar T-62T-40-1 auxiliary power unit

Nose glazing

▲ TROOP MOBILITY
The big doors of a Blackhawk allow infantry to dismount quickly.

Main undercarriage

M-23D .3 inch machine gun

Engine intake

General Electric T700-GE-700 turboshaft engine

Gear box

Titanium and glass-fiber rotor blades

helicopters nicknamed "gunships." The gunships were armed with 48 rockets and machine guns. The Bell H-1 Iroquois, which is universally known as the Huey, became the helicopter of the Vietnam War. Since 1958, some 9,440 Hueys have been built. The Bell AH-1 Cobra was the first dedicated attack helicopter and became the first helicopter to destroy tanks with anti-tank missiles from the air. The Boeing Vertol CH-47 Chinook twin-rotor helicopter was widely used to carry between 22 and 50 troops. By the end of the Vietnam War, the United States had lost nearly 5,000 helicopters.

The Soviet Union looked to the Cobra and developed the Mi-24 attack helicopter, which is known by NATO as the Hind. It saw action in Afghanistan between 1979 and 1989. Among the helicopters produced by the Soviet Union was the Mi-26 "Halo." It could carry 20 tonnes and was used to dump lead and concrete on the nuclear reactor at Chernobyl following its dramatic explosion in 1986.

The American Sikorsky H-60 Blackhawk troop-carrying helicopter and the McDonnell-Douglas H-64 Apache attack helicopter were used by the U.S. Army in the Gulf War in 1991.

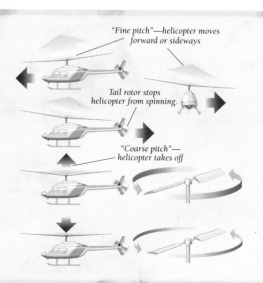

▶ HOW IT WORKS
A helicopter is sometimes known as a "rotary wing aircraft" because its main rotor can be tilted. This creates the current of air that flows over the wings to lift the aircraft into the sky. The angle of tilt of the rotor blades is called pitch, and "coarse pitch" is the sharp angle needed to lift the helicopter off the ground. The smaller tail rotor pushes against the rotation of the main rotor and so keeps the helicopter flying straight and level.

"Fine pitch"—helicopter moves forward or sideways

Tail rotor stops helicopter from spinning.

"Coarse pitch"—helicopter takes off

Key Dates

- 1500 Leonardo da Vinci sketches helicopter idea.

- 1907 September 29: first helicopter lifts a man off the ground into the air.

- 1914–1918 Austrians fly helicopters in World War I.

- 1942 American Sikorsky R-4 becomes first military helicopter.

- 1963 First true attack helicopter, the American Model 207 Sioux Scout.

- 1991 February 24: 300 helicopters used in Gulf War in the largest aerial assault in the history of aviation.

Doomsday Weapons

FOR CENTURIES WARS HAVE caused destruction on a large scale. However, it was not until the 20th century that the term "weapons of mass destruction" (WMD) came into use to describe chemical, biological, and nuclear weapons. Yet biological and chemical weapons are some of the oldest in existence.

In ancient times armies poisoned wells with dead animals or used disease-bearing rats to spread infection around besieged cities.

The first modern use of chemical weapons was in World War I. On April 22, 1915, the Germans released chlorine in support of an attack against the British and French at Ypres. In World War I most of the

▲ GAS DRILL
British soldiers wear anti-gas uniforms during a gas drill in 1939.

types of war gases that now exist were developed; these caused temporary choking and blistering on the skin or poisoned the blood. The blistering agent was called mustard gas because of its mustard-like smell.

By the end of World War I these gases had been contained in artillery shells. The shells were fired as part of a conventional high-explosive barrage when soldiers attacked.

▶ RESPIRATOR
These U.S. troops are equipped with the ABC-M17 respirator, which is a hood that fits over the head.

WEAPONS OF MASS DESTRUCTION

Nuclear, biological, and chemical weapons are particularly horrible because the damage they cause can be vast and almost open-ended. Viruses and germs used in biological weapons reproduce themselves and radiation after a nuclear explosion remains a hazard for centuries. These facts distinguish these weapons from conventional explosives, whose effect lasts for just one detonation.

None of the weapons of mass destruction has a localized effect like that of explosives. Wind and weather can cause spread the damage.

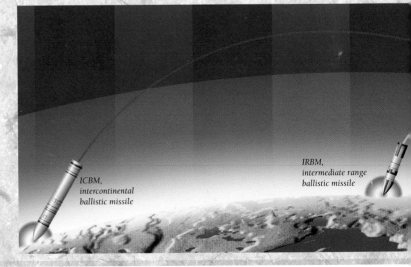

ICBM, intercontinental ballistic missile

IRBM, intermediate range ballistic missile

▼ FIRST ATOMIC BOMB
This bomb, codenamed "Little Boy," was dropped on Hiroshima on August 6, 1945. It had the power of 20,000 tonnes of TNT. It killed 78,150 people and destroyed 4 square miles of the city.

▲ BALLISTIC MISSILE
A U.S. ballistic missile lifts off during a test launch. With improved guidance, missiles are very accurate and capable of hitting small targets such as enemy missile silos.

The chemists of Nazi Germany produced the most effective chemical agent when they discovered nerve gas poisons. Called Tabun, Sarin, and Soman, they affected the human nervous system and killed within a few minutes. The Nazis never used this weapon, because they feared that the Allies also possessed it and would retaliate; in fact, the Allies did not have the weapon.

Iraq used mustard and nerve gases in 1984 during the Iran–Iraq war (1980–1988). They caused 40,000 deaths and injuries to the unprotected Iranian troops.

Atomic weapons were developed in the U.S. during World War II by a team of Europeans and Americans led by Robert Oppenheimer. They worked by releasing the energy from splitting the atom of uranium ore. The drive for this program had been the fear that German physicists might be developing a similar bomb. The first atomic bomb test took place in New Mexico on July 16, 1945. On August 6, an atomic bomb codenamed "Little Boy" was dropped on the Japanese city of Hiroshima. Three days later a device codenamed "Fat Man" was dropped on the city of Nagasaki. The explosions were the equivalent of the detonation of 20,000 tonnes of high explosives. In Hiroshima more than 70,000 people died or disappeared: in Nagasaki the figure was 40,000.

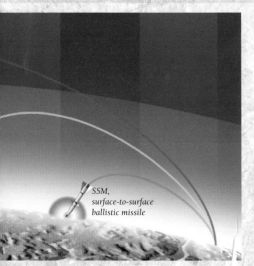

SSM, surface-to-surface ballistic missile

◀ MISSILES
Missiles are called "ballistic" because their flight is curved like that of a long-range shell.

▼ CRUISE MISSILE
An artist's impression of a nuclear-capable cruise missile as it homes in on its target.

Key Dates

- 1915 April 22: German chemical attack on Western Front.

- 1939–1945: German researchers develop nerve gases.

- 1945 August 6: atomic bomb dropped on Hiroshima.

- 1945 August 9: atomic bomb dropped on Nagasaki.

- 1949: USSR detonates its first atomic bomb.

- 1952: Britain detonates its first atomic bomb.

- 1966–1973: U.S. forces use Agent Orange defoliant in Vietnam.

Glossary

A

AA Antiaircraft, AA guns or AA missiles that are designed to shoot down aircraft.

AAM Air-to-air missile, missiles carried by aircraft for air combat.

AFV Armored Fighting Vehicle, tanks, APCs, and any vehicle protected by armor plate.

Amphibious Any vehicle capable of traveling on land and sea.

APC Armored personnel carrier, an AFV designed to carry an infantry squad.

Artillery Any large-calibre guns or cannons for land use.

B

Bolt-action A manually operated firing action, where the user moves the bolt to load a shell into the firing position, or breech.

Bomber A plane fitted with external racks, or internal bays, which allow it to carry bombs for attacks on enemy ground or sea targets. "Bomber" is also used by the British Royal Navy to describe nuclear missile armed submarines.

C

Cannon Originally the guns carried by wooden-hulled warships and used by armies in the field up to the mid-19th century, now the guns fitted to combat aircraft.

CBU Cluster bomb unit, aircraft bomb that contains smaller bombs (sub-munitions) which scatter over a wide area.

D

Depth charge An explosive charge in a cylindrical container fitted with a fuse that detonates it at a set depth below the surface of the sea. It was used in world wars I and II and was designed to sink or damage submarines.

Dynamite A powerful explosive devised in Sweden by Alfred Nobel in 1863.

E

Ejection Seat The crew seats on a jet-powered combat plane which are fitted with a rocket that fires them clear of the aircraft if it is damaged and likely to crash. The parachute deploys and the ejection seat can be discarded as the crew float down.

F

Flak German World War II abbreviation for Flieger Abwehr Kanonen, or antiaircraft guns. It is now widely used in place of "anti-aircraft gun".

FPB Fast patrol boat, a small craft armed with light guns, missiles or torpedoes.

G

GPMG General purpose machine gun, a gun that can be mounted on a tripod for long-range fire.

Ground Strafing Attacks by fighter planes against targets on the ground such as infantry and trucks.

H

H.M.S. His/Her Majesty's Ship, the title of warships in service of the British Royal Navy.

I

ICBM Intercontinental ballistic missile, a nuclear missile that can travel huge distances to remote targets.

IR Infrared, the invisible heat from animate and inanimate objects. IR can also be used like an invisible flashlight for illumination.

IRBM Intermediate-range ballistic missile, a nuclear missile with a shorter range than an ICBM.

K

Kamikaze Japanese for "divine wind" from a legendary storm in the 13th century that saved Japan from invasion. The name was used in World War II for ships and aircraft sent on suicide attacks against U.S. and Allied warships in 1945.

L

Landing craft A boat designed to carry troops and vehicles and land them on sloping shores by using hinged doors in its bows or bow-mounted ramps.

LMG Light machine gun, a weapon usually found in an infantry squad or section.

M

MAG *Mitrailleuse a Gaz* (Belgium), a GPMG developed after World War II and widely used throughout the world.

Minesweeper A ship often made with a non-magnetic hull and equipped to detect and destroy enemy sea mines.

N

Napalm An incendiary bomb dropped by aircraft which uses thickened gasoline.

P

Panzer Literally "armor," the abbreviation of the World War II *Panzerkampfwagen*—armored war vehicle, the German word for a tank.

PE Plastic explosives, gelignite developed in World War II in a form that can be shaped like putty. SEMTEX is a plastic explosive.

R

RAF Royal Air Force, the British air force.

Reconnaissance The act of finding out anything that will help in battle, such as numbers of soldiers.

S

SAM Surface-to-air missile, an AA missile which can be a lightweight weapon fired by one person from the shoulder or long-range missile.

SATCOM Satellite communications, radio signals transmitted via an orbiting satellite over vast distances.

SP Gun Self-propelled gun, artillery mounted on an AFV chassis which protects the crew and ensures their mobility.

SSM Surface-to-surface missile, any missile launched from the ground against another target also on the ground.

Stuka Sturzkampfflugzeug, World War II German literally "diving warplane," but widely associated with the Ju 87 dive bomber.

Submersible Any vehicle capable of travelling under water, primarily submarines.

T

TNT Trinitrotoluene, a powerful explosive.

U

U-Boat German submarine in world wars I and II.

USAAF United States Army Air Force, American Air Force in World War II.

USMC United States Marine Corps.

U.S.S. United States Ship, the title of American warships.

W

WP White Phosphorus, a material that produces thick white smoke and causes severe burns. Used in shells and grenades.

Index

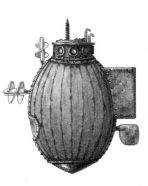